Sweet
highs, lows & mystic glows

Sweet
highs, lows & mystic glows

Shereen Baird

Spirit Time Press
Viroqua, WI

Sweet: highs, lows & mystic glows

Copyright © 2021 by Shereen Baird

All rights reserved. No portion of this book may be reproduced in any form without permission from the author.

Cover and interior design by Gabriel Newton Simmons

ISBN: 978-0-9990289-1-9

For my 20-year-old self, to whom I promised I'd write this book. And for YOU reading it now. May my words put some jewels in your pocket.

Contents

Author's Note xi

Chapter 1:
GROWING UP 1

Chapter 2:
THE CALL TO ADVENTURE 13

Chapter 3:
THE SEARCH FOR LOVE & ROMANCE 31

Chapter 4:
THE SEARCH FOR PERSIA 45

Chapter 5:
THE SEARCH FOR MOTHERHOOD 53

Chapter 6:
THE SEARCH FOR HEALING, PEACE & PURPOSE 71

Chapter 7:
THE SEARCH FOR ANSWERS TO THE BIG QUESTIONS 91

Chapter 8:
LIFE'S WISDOM & WHAT I'VE LEARNED 109

Chapter 9:
WHERE I AM NOW 133

Chapter 10:
BLESSINGS TO YOU 147

Resources 151
Acknowledgments 153
Index of Poems 155

Life Moves

As Life moves and does its thing,
my heart beats and longs to sing.

To heed the call and take the plunge,
to soak up life like a thirsty sponge.

To speak the truth from within my soul,
to trust and make peace my mighty goal.

Author's Note

"There are no good or bad experiences, only experiences"
Edward (a shaman I met in Italy)

At age 20, I found myself reflecting on my life thus far as a half Scottish, half Iranian girl growing up in the rough streets of Glasgow, Scotland and in the small town troubles of Northern Ireland. I was blown away by both the pain and beauty of it all. I remember feeling like I'd already lived a lifetime of experiences but also feeling young and awed by the whole lifetime that lay ahead. I felt excited, curious and terrified all at once. This is when the desire to write a book about my life was born.

All I knew back then is that 'the book' was due around my 40th birthday, and that here I stood between the history of the past and the mystery of the future. I was feeling the push of the pain and pull of the call to adventure, driven by a strong desire for Answers, Love, Home. This was the rocket fuel that sent me off around the globe and took me on a tour of my inner worlds and the otherly realms of existence.

Why I Had to Write this Book

I wrote this book to keep a promise to my 20-year-old self. I wrote this for my family and friends to fill them in on my whereabouts over the years and the journey I've been on.

I wrote this to share my experiences, life lessons and the wisdom I've gleaned, in the hope it will entertain, stir hope, and inspire whoever feels drawn to read it. I wrote this to make a dream come true and to have all my poems gathered in a somewhat coherent manner in one place.

I wrote this to shine light on my past, so I could drop the heavy boulders and keep the jewels, and move forward with a lighter, brighter sack. I named this book *Sweet* because Shereen means 'sweet' in Persian.

The Process of Writing

When I first decided I'd write this book, I had never read a book, not willingly anyway, and not from cover to cover—not for educational reasons or pleasure. In fact, growing up I struggled with reading and writing. In my early 30s I found out I had 'dyslexia', which I reckon is just a fancy word for saying that my brain has different superpowers than the average Joe. The first book I ever read, at age 23, was an autobiography in Spanish and the first poem I ever wrote was in French a few years later.

At age 33, I wrote my first spontaneous rhyming poems (see pages 105-108). Or better put, these poems wrote me. In the years that followed I wrote more and more spontaneous poems (most of which are in the latter part of this book). These poems reflected my moment-to-moment experiences, my observations and the wisdom that wanted to be revealed through me.

As my love for writing poems grew, I made the crazy decision to write about my whole life thus far in rhyming poetry, just 2 years before this book's long-awaited deadline! I say crazy, because at times I wished I didn't need to make it all rhyme, so I could more fully express what I wanted to say. But this decision also meant I had a form to work with, which helped me to not ramble on, allowing me to keep it short, simple and straight to the point. So in the end I'm glad I chose to make it rhyme.

There are two types of poems in this book, ones that relay my story through time, the others are timeless.

Writing About the Past

In my early-mid 20's I tried to write some pages, but I didn't yet have the skills to look back into the past and remain anchored in the present. It almost always resulted in me being only able to see it from a negative angle, writing just made me depressed. I wrote the majority of this book at age 39, where thanks to years of meditation, and study of my heart and mind, I was able to see my past in a whole new light.

Writing about my life has been both challenging and truly healing and rewarding. It's like my 20-year-old self knew that by embarking on this mission to write about my past, from this future stand point, I'd see it for what it truly was—magical. The process of reflecting and writing has led me to heal old wounds and harvest the lessons and blessings of my journey, so I can now share them with others.

Sharing this Book with Others

Sharing this book with others is requiring that I embody my Scottish Braveheart and shout 'Freedom!' Sharing creative work in general can be scary, sharing personal adventures, trials, tragedies, victories, joys etc. evokes a whole new level of scary... It's also liberating.

While the act of writing has resulted in the birth of this book into existence through my body-mind-spirit (from the conception of the idea to the completed book) the step towards sharing it caused, in a sense, the book to give birth me. This took me by surprise.

I was unexpectedly met by a 'coming out of the womb' experience, like being thrust down the birth canal, accompanied by fear and Love, no other way to go but out! Pushed through a tight hole, out into a new place, feeling exposed, naked and vulnerable. Yet freed from what had become a tight space.

Reflecting on the Future

They say life begins at 40. It truly feels like a new beginning for me, a new chapter. Writing and completing this book has been, in a way, a ritualistic letting go *and* an embracing of my past. As a result I feel like I have more space for what the future has in store for me.

While I'm aware I have a say in much of what my future will look like, by the choices I make, and where I put my focus and attention, I also know much of what's to come is out of my control. I could live till I'm 80, which would mean I still have a whole half of life ahead of me, or not.

What matters is that I live each day like it's my last and continue to follow my heart, open to what experiences will come in the form of people, places, lessons and blessings.

I stand in gratitude for the dark, the light and everything in-between. For the mystery in the history, the mystery in what's to come and for the precious present moment, that place in time that allows us to touch the timeless and be at one with Life itself—the place I plan to spend the majority of my future.

Join me for a deep dive into the oceans of emotions and a high jump into the skies of the wise...

—Shereen Baird
February 2021

The Idea to Write this Book

Four decades of this lifetime
have passed me by,
the idea to write this book came
when I was 20 and high.

High on drugs and youthfulness,
high on the mystery.
The idea was, when I was 40,
I'd write about my life's history.

Being aged 20 meant half of the book
had already been written.
The latter half was mine to fill,
so I got inspired to leave Britain.

Throughout these pages
I share some stories from my head,
stories from what came before
and from ones that lay ahead.

Of experiences that took me
on inner and outer explorations,
in search of beauty, peace
and the truth of our foundations.

After the facts and stories,
I share some wisdom from above,
that came to guide me, calm me,
remind me—we're all made of Love.

Chapter 1
GROWING UP

Made in Iran in 1980

SCOTLAND/IRAN

My mum is from Glasgow, Scotland.
My dad was from Tehran, Iran.
He came to her city to study and met her there—
a bonus to his plan.

They married and it was time
for mum to meet the family abroad.
But 1980 was not a prime time to go to Iran,
why they went then is odd.

The Islamic Revolution had not long ended,
banished Ayatollah Khomeini had returned,
and the Iran-Iraq war was in the air.
Nonetheless it seemed my dad was keen
to be with his family and show off his wife,
he needed to be there.

They had planned to visit for just a few weeks,
but the chaos had them trapped.
No one was allowed to leave the country,
so they had to just adapt.

On top of being stuck in Iran at that time,
my mum's grandma passed away.
Trapped and grieving, unable to get home,
I wonder did she pray?

Despite the commotion, mum did meet the family,
and got to see some sights.
And it turns out that I was conceived there,
a blessing in which she still delights.

The Glasgow Kiss

SCOTLAND

I grew up in Scotland,
in the most populated city—Glasgow.
On a bleak street were poverty, drink, drugs
and violence were on show.

Dodging bricks and bottles
from frequent gang fights was the norm,
strange, because Scottish hearts
truly are tender, loving, and warm.

We lived in a flat
attached to many other identical ones,
our shared front and back yards
growing trash by the tons.

I shared a room with my brother David,
who's 5 years younger than me.
I wasn't always the kindest big sister,
I'm sure that he'd agree.

I had some wonderful friends from my neighbourhood,
and another crew from school.
And of course there were the 'other kids',
whose idea of fun were rather cruel.

Being half Iranian,
I was occasionally a target for racism.
"Get back to Pakistan!" they'd say,
which I received as hurtful criticism.

I went to non-denominational schools
and in primary school I was rather shy.
By the time I was in secondary school
I was a bit of a rebel and quite often high.

I witnessed the gang fights
and got my ass kicked many times.
I joined in the teenage shenanigans
and committed a good few crimes.

At high school we got to go to Paris and Amsterdam,
to visit art galleries with our art class.
I got drunk on the boat to France, ran into a wall,
nearly broke my neck, and landed on my ass.

We lived near Rangers Football Club,
so there were often football fans about.
We'd watch their cars to make some cash,
then buy some booze and hangout.

Every neighbourhood has its chippy,
where you get your fried fish and chips.
I loved the rolls-n-fritters and batter Mars Bars
with a can of Irn-Bru, what a banging mix!

Glasgow is known for its strong
non-understandable dialect.
For its rude boy attitude and heavy party scene,
with its depressing side effect.

I was there until I was 15,
by then a pro drinker, smoker and fighter.
I left with a dialect people didn't understand,
I'm now a calm, kind, multilingual writer!

Head butting our fellow humans
is a well know Glasgow trait,
known as the Glasgow Kiss.
Although my upbringing was often gloom,
the real kiss this town gave me
was the strength to follow my bliss.

My Scottish Relatives

My mum has always been my rock,
her voice the sweetest thing.
She often has a jolly face
and you'll often hear her sing.

My brother David was super cute
and has grown into a smart, handsome guy.
I am blessed to have him in my life
and I'm sorry I made him cry.

My grandparents and uncle
lived at the end of our street.
We'd visit often, especially Sundays,
to play cards and eat.

My mum had three brothers
and I had a few great aunts and uncles too.
There were not that many cousins
and I grew up with just a few.

My cousins were, and still are,
my bosom buddy friends.
We had lots of fun, and we'd fight,
but we'd always make amends.

All in all, a close, loving crew,
to which my bonds are strong indeed.
Their loving presence made me feel
wrapped in woollen woven tweed.

Just like most families,
we had our brokenness and madness.
Some alcohol abuse, a bit of violence
and our joint sadness.

I was really close to my nana,
she took me on her bingo trips.
I'd ask her lots of deep questions
over some fish and chips.

She was my beloved mentor
whom I'd share my secrets with.
She smoked long menthol cigarettes
and her family name was Smith.

My Baba Star

My dad, my baba,
my mama's prince Ali,
was a fine young man.
A handsome dude,
light skinned and blue eyed,
despite being from Iran.

I loved to hang with my baba,
he'd take me to the local park.
We'd draw each other and munch
on pistachios until it got dark.

The day after my 10th birthday
my mama sat me on her knee,
to tell me my baba passed away,
to which I made a mournful plea.

When I asked all the adults
"What do you mean he's dead?"
"Where did he go?"
All gave different answers,
"he's a star", "he's an angel,"
"sorry sweet heart, I don't know."

Confused, in disbelief,
full of rage and anger,
I was totally broken-hearted.
My desire and search for
peace, truth and sacred
knowledge started.

He was such a wonderful father
who showered me with Love.
I know he's always been with me,
sending guidance from above.

Good Ould Ballycastle Hey

NORTHERN IRELAND

Mum met a new Scotch-Irish man,
who she's still with today.
And because of the violence in our street,
we had to move away.

I didn't want to move,
because all my friends were there.
They threw me a surprise party at school,
sending me off in love and care.

We moved to Northern Ireland,
to a lovely seaside town.
It took a while to find our feet
and get settled down.

This was a tough year,
not long after we arrived my beloved nana died.
Meeting her lifeless body was hard,
I cried and cried and cried.

Soon after, my dog Buster of 9 years
got real ill.
On my 16th birthday
the vet had no choice but to kill.

Although I had my ups and downs
with mum's new man,
it's thanks to him we moved,
and a new life for me began.

Starting a new school
and meeting new friends were hard at first.
Day one I punched a guy,
in an inappropriate outburst.

As the heaviness and newness settled,
I found some great new pals.
I started to really like the place, the school,
the beach and these new guys n gals.

I wasn't associated with any religion,
when I was growing up.
My new school was Catholic,
and I had to try this out, to fill my curious cup.

My first job
was taking a greyhound dog for a run.
Then I worked as a dishwasher,
with kind workmates who were fun.

To my surprise, my little bro Sean
was born when I was seventeen.
He's an adorable wee fella,
who loves the colour green.

GROWING UP

The Lammas Fair would come to town,
every single year.
Bringing dulse, yellowman and honeycomb,
fun and good cheer.

My relationship with weed and booze accelerated
and I tried some 'harder stuff.'
It wasn't long before this reached the stage—
'enough is enough.'

And after getting into a bad fight,
that had the cops involved,
I dropped the rude-boy attitude,
and transformed and evolved.

On occasion I experienced
the Northern Ireland conflict in my town.
Petrol bombs, cops with guns, shields, tanks,
and the townsfolk with an angry frown.

A petrol bomb put through the letter box
of the house down stairs, thankfully didn't explode.
And we once got evacuated from work,
because of a bomb scare in the shop across the road.

I got engaged to my first love, Sean,
we moved into a wee bungalow.
We went to Greece and Turkey together,
and we did a bungee jump, you know.

After 4 years,
our relationship began to fall apart.
It was time to go our separate ways,
ouch, a broken heart.

Mysterious Dreams

*Before we go any further
I want to share one of the secrets,
I'd only shared with my nana.
It was about a dream I had about my dad,
about two months after he died
and went to Nirvana.*

I was in a huge empty warehouse,
and I spotted my dad
far away over there.
We ran towards each other,
he picked me up, I kicked and screamed,
and he hugged me like a bear.

With tears running down my face I said
"They all told me you were dead,
tell me it's not true!"
"I'm sorry sweetheart it's true,
but I will always be by your side"
he said "and I'll never stop loving you."

The next day I felt even worse,
as he too had confirmed that I'd never
see him again in his physical form.
But knowing that he was still there,
somewhere, loving me, helped me
to move through this tragic storm.

I told my nana about this dream
and asked her to promise me
to also visit me in my dreams.
She promised and she *did* come.
She got to visit us in our new town
after-all, it seems.

Chapter 2

It was the Lammas Fair and the town
was crowded. I and all the people
were walking towards the beach.
Across the crowd I spotted her—
the only one going the other way,
I tried to get to her but she was out of reach.

Stunning, her hair golden,
skin tanned, she had an almighty glow
emanating from within her.
I woke with a smile upon my heart,
I felt her and the mystery
within me stir.

Chapter 2
THE CALL TO ADVENTURE

J'ai Treize Ans

CANADA

Now here I was, aged 20,
the year the idea to write this book was born.
Ready to participate and watch the stories unfold,
while munching on popcorn.

Not long after my breakup in Ireland,
mum showed me an ad in a magazine
"Here's an opportunity to go to Canada
on a work exchange, Shereen."

I jumped at the chance of this free,
2 month long trip.
I was soon off with 20 other youngsters
and a few dudes in leadership.

We went to Montreal
where many folk speak French.
We visited Niagara Falls,
which I admired from a nearby bench.

Montreal is full of wonderful winding
outdoor staircases that line the streets.
Poutine—fries, cheese curds and gravy—
is the street food everyone eats.

The only French I remembered
was how to say "my name is …"
And "J'ai treize ans, I'm 13"
which got puzzled looks—gee-whiz!

I stayed in a basement, with two cute
Irish girls, in a Canadian family's home.
We were given some rules about this and that,
but we were pretty much free to roam.

THE CALL TO ADVENTURE

Throughout, I had a job working for Air Canada—
helping to make ID cards
for all their employees.
For all my hard work, they offered me
a free plane ticket to go anywhere!
To which I said "yes please!"

Being 20, I was feeling
young, free and single,
exited about opportunities
to go explore and mingle.

I went on a few romantic dates,
had pleasant strolls along the seashore.
I watched Montreal's ice hockey
team play and boogied on the dance floor.

One night while out at a club
I took a drug I was offered there.
I had a terribly bad trip
that rapidly sent me to despair.

Homesickness and depression
soon kicked in,
and into driftwood mode I went,
without a grin...

Driftwood Mode

BACK IN IRELAND

Back in Ireland at my mums place,
I was totally lost and sad.
I had no idea what was happening to me,
was I going mad?

Total disconnect from life,
I had nothing left to give.
Seeing only a bleak past and future,
I didn't want to live.

All my pain from the past arose to the surface
for me to see, feel, and heal.
The doc gave me a pill that interrupted this pattern,
which is really not ideal.

However, it did as he said it would,
after 21 days I started to feel better.
I was relieved and felt I'd been released
from a debilitatingly tight fetter.

With a little sparkle back in my eyes
and a little spring in my step,
I was ready to give life a shot again,
and take that next small step.

I had a free airplane ticket
to go anywhere in the world!
This helped me get into a better state,
and I totally unfurled.

Shaggy

HAWAII

I chose to go to Honolulu, Hawaii,
and was excited to go surf and splash.
I worked for a bit as a hotel receptionist
to earn some spending cash.

On arrival in Honolulu, I was given
a gorgeous necklace of flowers.
I was grinning from ear to ear,
and felt I had new super powers.

I was excited to see the palm trees
and feel the tropical sunny vibes outside.
But after days and days of travelling,
I was feeling rather fried.

A kind Hawaiian family offered to drive me
to my hostel and helped me with my bag,
I was filled with awe and gratitude at this
kind act, that helped ease my jet-lag.

The next morning I was eager to explore.
Everyone I passed said aloha-hello.
I had pancakes for breakfast and called
mum to tell her I'd made it not long ago.

Before setting off to explore some more,
I sat on a wall near the cafe to take in the view
and smoke a cigarette.
While taking it all in, a really tall dude
on his skateboard rocked up—
this is how me and Shaggy met.

Shaggy was from California.
He was homeless,

and often slept on the beach.
He offered to show me around
and I was sure he had
something useful to teach.

He introduced me to the locals,
and to the movies and fireworks
on the beach on the weekends.
We went on hikes and he showed me
the gorgeous sights, and in no time,
we became bosom buddy friends.

On the first day, stoned, I got
myself a tattoo, a Japanese symbol
that was supposed to mean 'smooth.'
Later I found out it actually means
'slide', which I had to accept,
as it's something I can't remove.

The area where I stayed was near
the beach, it had a Paradise feel
and was adorned with palm trees.
I tried surfing, joined local parties and
BBQ's, and immersed myself in this
whole new world overseas.

Me and Shaggy went on a mission
to pick magic mushrooms,
which he would usually swap for weed.
Back on the beach we had mushroom tea,
and I turned into Spiderman
and took off at top speed.

Shaggy would walk me back to
my hostel every night and would
be waiting for me every morning.
And although there was no
romance between us,
I found him sweet and charming.

I still had six days to go
before my flight back home,
and I ran out of money.
And Shaggy was upset
'cause I'd kissed his friend,
"oh shit this isn't funny."

I sat on a step and cried,
and a young Hawaiian man came over
and asked me what was wrong.
He gave me a loaf of bread and snacks,
suggested a job at the hostel,
and ushered me along.

But I didn't need a job in the end,
as Shaggy's friend offered
me food and a place to stay.
And soon Shaggy became my
friend again, and stayed with me
until my last aloha day.

I Want to Learn your Language

SOUTHERN IRELAND

Back in Northern Ireland,
I went on a road trip with friends,
we headed south.
I didn't go back home with them,
I went to Galway City to live,
which I heard of by word of mouth.

I found a room to rent and a job
in the city center, as a waitress in
a 4 star hotel restaurant.
My colleagues were from all over
the globe, all there to learn English,
I thought "this is what I want."

"I want to go to your county
and learn your language."
I was sold on this idea.
But how and when should I go,
where could I go,
"Should I start with South Korea?"

I wanted to learn both French
and Spanish so I was on a mission
to go to Spain and France.
I was ready to leave Ireland
and super keen to give
this new dream a chance.

It turned out four of my Spanish
work pals were heading back to
Spain in a van and had a spare seat.
We were soon off driving down through
Ireland, and through France,
passing street after street.

They were all from different
parts of Spain and they asked
me where I wanted to go.
I said the first big city,
they said Barcelona, I said
 "great, drop me there please bro."

I didn't know a word of Spanish
and I learned three words;
gracias, estupendo and si, on the road.
Thank you, great and yes,
a handy trio to get me started,
until I found my new humble abode.

Picking up the Lingo

SPAIN

My van companions dropped
me off in the city center,
and we said our farewells.
I got swept up in
a giant puppet festival
while searching for hotels.

I remember feeling thrilled
but also terrified, aware I couldn't
communicate, and I was all alone.
I acknowledged the sun was shining
and primed my self
to step into the mystery of the unknown.

A week later I found a live-in nanny
deal with a family from Ecuador,
taking care of their little boy.
I shared a room there with the
daughter and a couple of Latin girls,
whom getting to know was a real joy.

My roommate from Peru gave
me my first Spanish lesson, how to
conjugate the verb 'follar—to fuck'
She proceeded, Yo follo (I fuck),
tu follas (you fuck) and so on,
I couldn't believe my luck!

I lived right beside a gorgeous park,
which had a boat pond, a zoo,
and many sweet spots to chill.
I spent lots of time there, snoozing,
eating, relaxing and learning
my Spanish language skill.

Not being able to communicate and
having no one to have a conversation with,
was hard in the beginning.
But after just a few months
I started dreaming in Spanish,
this is when I knew I was winning.

Discovering Yoga

After a few months in Spain,
I began missing my family
and grieving the life I once had.
Change, loss,
and directionlessness showed up,
I lost ground and felt quite sad.

I saw an ad for a Yoga class,
that would be led in English
by a Scottish lady.
I was intrigued to meet her
and give Yoga a try,
"it could be what I needed, maybe?"

It was exactly what I needed,
and the effects were profound
and instant.
I was in love with this practice,
'twas my new body-mind-heart
cuddling assistant!

The yoga teacher was and still is
a mentor of mine
and I am grateful for her in every way.
I fell in love with yoga,
a gift I turn to and practice even now,
every single day.

Dubious Jobs

I had been baby sitting little Jose
through the night,
in exchange for a place to stay.
Until his mum quit her job
and no longer needed me,
and so asked if I could pay.

I needed a 'proper' job and
so took myself off to the
immigration office to get papers.
I was informed I was already
a European citizen, if only
I'd read the newspapers!

I really did need to find work,
as I was very low on cash, but my
Spanish was still not that great.
I tried the Irish, Scottish, English
bars, but wrong season,
they said I'd have to wait.

I got some dodgy cash in hand
jobs in a few cafe bars until I
picked up the lingo a bit better.
A girl I met kindly helped me
translate my CV into Spanish,
and wrote me a cover letter.

At one point I had only 50 cents,
some pasta and some
ketchup to my name.
So I worked one day behind
a bar where prostitutes
and sleezy men came.

That same day I found a job in El Pintor,
a snazzy traditional restaurant,
they needed an English speaker.
My colleagues became my new
family members, and we drank
wine together by the beaker.

It was a fun place to work but the
hours really sucked, from 11am-1am,
with a few hours break between.
I got into siesta time, taking naps in
the park, but after one year of this,
I needed a change of scene.

Between jobs I had a bike accident
that threw me in the air,
and put me in intensive care.
I fractured my elbow in two
places and had to get surgery,
so they could put 2 pins in there.

At this time I was babysitting Jose
again and his older siblings,
while their mum went to Ecuador.
But it turns out his sister had to
babysit me instead. She lovingly helped me
bathe and go to the store.

I got a new job working as
a shop assistant in a ceramic craft
shop, surrounded by local art.
And I studied a teaching English
language course. This is where
my teaching career got its start.

I quit my job at the art shop
and was making a living teaching
English in groups and one-to-ones.

This was an interesting endeavor,
as I had to improve my own
English grammar and spelling by the tons!

Fiesta and Siesta Time

Barcelona is a wild city,
there are fiestas and festivals
most days of the year.
Fullmoon parties and nudist
beaches where you're sure to
be offered 'cervesa'—beer.

People are nuts with fireworks
in Spain. Once one exploded just
inches from my face.
My brother and his friend
had to army crawl
to get to a safer place.

In Barcelona, like in other big
European cities its
common to get robbed.
I once watched a guy
get punched on the nose,
I'm sure that throbbed.

The architecture around the city
is incredibly impressive, with
Gaudi buildings everywhere.
Las Ramblas is a busy tourist street
full of performers and human
statues with a frozen stare.

The majority of my friends were
from Latin America, a few Spanish,
French and Moroccans too.

We drank sangria, danced salsa,
ate paella and hung out by the
beach, these guys were my crew.

One day a few of us planned to go
ski in the Pyrenees, but in the end they
couldn't come, so I went alone.
My first time skiing and I ended up
needing rescued on the black ski slope!
I was lucky I didn't break a bone.

My gay pals from work loved
to take me out on the town
to the gay party scenes.
They were often over the top
erotic and wild, and chock full
of sexy-man-queens.

I thoroughly enjoyed living in this
wonderful wacky city and meeting
all these great new friends.
However the constant fiesta
meant I had to do siesta often,
and take time out to cleanse.

Behind Bars

PERU

I went to Peru with
my Peruvian flatmate,
I stayed at her family's home.
Her area in Lima was sketchy,
the shops were behind bars,
so she told me not to roam.

I stood out like a sore thumb,
the only white, blue-eyed person
from outer space about.
Everyone overcharged me, except the
bus driver,"hey blue eyes jump on free"
he'd shout.

We visited Machu Picchu,
what an amazing sight!
And explored the Cosco Region.
I hung out with the locals,
which I love to do,
and they hung with me, a Glaswegian.

Danish Rye

DENMARK

I met a new Danish friend in
Spanish class, she invited me to
visit her in Denmark.
We visited Freetown Christiania,
once an abandoned military base,
now emerged from the dark.

We toured the cities and
her local zone, and
munched on danish rye.
I had tons of fun playing
with her baby daughter,
what a sweetie pie.

Kundalini Surprise

SPAIN

One day, after a tough
downer, coming up
from an all time low,
I was handed a leaflet
to a free mystical music gig,
I thought "why not go?"

It was going to start in just 10
minutes, so I found myself a seat
and got myself cosy.
I had no idea what I was there to
watch, but I was relaxed and curious,
not pushy or nosy.

The room filled with about 50 people,
the lights dimmed and the band
made there way to the stage.
They looked like they were from India,
with dots on their foreheads—
each had the presence of a sage.

They sat on the floor and formed a
crescent moon, with their exotic
instruments and mic's at hand.
As soon as they began I was
hooked and mesmerized,
this was no ordinary band.

Soon I found myself standing and
swaying, and then dancing
like I'd never done before.
I was totally sober, on my own,
having the best time of my life,
I wanted more and more.

After a good solid hour of dancing,
super super hard, I got pretty tired
and had to sit myself back down.
When, surprisingly, I felt an energy so
intense rise up my spine and into my head,
I thought I might disappear or drown.

It felt sooo good, yet terrifying,
I had no idea what was going on,
it was too much, I wanted it to stop.
After a few moments I was blissfully
back in the room, a seed of joy had
hatched, and shown me an almighty crop.

After the show, I bought the album
'Sangeet Lahari Inner Joy', said thanks,
and joyfully jumped back on my bike.
I cycled for miles and miles along the
beach, with no hands late into the night,
in a state that was dreamlike.

It wasn't until about 15 years after this
that the word "Kundalini" arrived in my
world, and I discovered more about this.
Maybe that's what happened that night,
this energy began to awaken in me.
It was my first experience of such pure bliss.

Chapter 3
THE SEARCH FOR LOVE AND ROMANCE

The Sweet Mint Tea

MOROCCO

Soon after arriving in Barcelona,
I had a boyfriend, Hafid from Morocco,
he once rescued my robbed backpack.
We visited his hometown near Tangier,
where I saw a donkey
carrying eggs on its back.

The house where I stayed had no
plumbing, I had to have a bucket
bath with water from a nearby well.
We went to Meknes city for a
wedding, were I had a delightful
hamam bath to rid me of my smell.

The sweet mint tea they drink there is
so good and family meals are intimate—
everyone eats from one big plate.
I learned a little Arabic and Berber,
and the folk would repeatedly tell me
to eat, eat, eat—so I ate.

Back in Barcelona, this
relationship soon went south,
and things got way out of hand.
Obsessive chaos turned to
violence, so I had to make
a firm 'stay away' demand.

Feeling fragile and not wanting
to break hearts or have my heart
broken, I proceeded with care.
I dated a few Latin boys and as
soon as love entered the picture
on either side, I'd run like a hare.

Latin Boys

SPAIN

I was Walter's first love it seemed,
he was head over heels.
But I felt he was too young.
He told me that love songs now
made sense to him and made
me a CD that was beautifully sung.

At one point I had a crush on
an Argentinian guy and I once
dated a guy from Chile.
But around now was also
when I began dreaming of
France so dating seemed silly.

Nevertheless, I really love how affectionate
and romantic Latin boys can be,
and how they like to dance.
I thought "a kiss or two on a park
bench won't do any harm, it doesn't
have to be a big romance."

But kisses are dangerous and
I was soon in love with skydiving,
skateboarder Fredy from Venezuela.
We had wild adventures together.
We once slept under a street lamp
that looked like an umbrella.

He was aware of my plans to go
learn French and didn't want to
stop me from going after this dream.
Because of his immigration status,
there was no way he could get on board
with this scheme.

I was confused about what to do,
I wanted to be with him but I also
wanted to go live in France.
So we agreed to try a long
distance relationship, so we could
continue our new found romance.

He helped me with my bags and
accompanied me to the bus station,
were we said our goodbyes.
He waved me off as the bus left
the depot, and I waved back,
feeling sad, with tears in my eyes.

Alone with the Mice

FRANCE

Before leaving Barcelona I'd met
a friend of a friend who lived in
Toulouse—the city I was moving to.
So after a few nights in a hostel,
I called him to see if he could help me
out and share with me what he knew.

He was renting a room with other
Peruvian folks and managed to sort
me out with a floor bed at their place.
Plus, he put me in touch with a friend
who gave me a job at his Peruvian-French
restaurant, which I embraced.

The house was small, dirty and hectic,
there were four Peruvians living there,
one young girl and three older guys.
Very soon the girl, who was illegally
living in France got caught stealing
underwear and got deported—how unwise!

So now I was alone with these three
drunken dudes who ate ceviche often
and danced salsa all night long.
One night they squabbled and
the head of the house kicked the
others out—they no longer got along.

Then the one guy left decided he
was going to Peru for a month or two,
so this left me alone with all the mice.
It was time to find a better place to stay,
a better job and a place to study French,
I really needed some advice.

Teaching English and Learning French

I was discovered by this angel lady
who was super keen to help me out,
and shocked at where I'd been living.
She hooked me up with teaching
English opportunities, and a place
to stay—she was kind and giving.

She found me a room to rent with
a French family, where I helped
their daughter with her English exams.
And got me a job teaching English
in primary schools, working with
her and her teaching programs.

I later had other teaching
opportunities with teenagers,
and with kids with disabilities.
I taught kids who were blind, deaf and
in wheelchairs, they were super inspiring
and had super power capabilities.

I also taught adults who worked for
Airbus, an aerospace corporation
who manufacture flying machines.
The English I taught them was
'business English' unlike the stuff I'd
been teaching the young ones and teens.

I found a weekly French class, were I
wrote my first poem and I later studied
part-time at university.
I had classmates from Japan, Ethiopia,
Taiwan, Ukraine, Russia, Argentina.
I was at home in this diversity.

The Doom Zone

The long distance relationship with
Fredy in Barcelona was not easy,
it was really not the best.
I visited him, he visited me, and we
met in Ibiza, but our relationship
was soon put to rest.

The chaotic rocky start in France, the
grief from leaving Spain and this
break up, sent me into doom.
I was back at the doctor seeking
relief, as I could not get rid of
this intolerable feeling of gloom.

This time the doc gave me a pill
that destroyed my thyroid, made me loose weight
and made my hair fall out!
I was depressed, not functioning well,
and confused at what was happening—
what was this about?

Life had been swept from under my feet,
I was full of despair,
and my head was full of negativity.
I was consumed by dark
thoughts and feelings
that held me in captivity.

At one point I got on my knees
and prayed for the first time to a God
that I wasn't sure was there or not.
I asked "if you're there, hold me and tell me
everything is going to be alright."
"Why not give this a shot," I thought.

I spent some weeks in recovery, no work
or play or trying to figure anything out,
I needed to grieve and rest.
It wasn't long before the old doors closed
and new doors opened,
and I was feeling refreshed and blessed.

Mon Mari d'Algérie Abdenour

I spent lots of time hanging out by
La Garonne river and indulging
in the French culture, music and food.
I tried frogs legs, Cassoulet (stewed
duck, beans and pork), crepes and cheese
that smelled bad but tasted real good.

One day while out exploring the
city, a cute guy sitting on a wall,
asked me for the time.
We got chatting and I joined him
at a nearby cafe were I drank
soda flavoured with mint and lime.

I bumped into this handsome young
man in the weeks that followed
and soon a spark became a flame.
We hung out in the shisha bar,
smoking hookah and drinking mint tea,
playing an exciting smoking game.

He introduced me to his friends
and we visited various cities
Paris, Carcassonne, Lyon and such.
He didn't drink or do drugs,
exactly what I needed, as I had been
doing that shit too much.

We enjoyed strolls in the park
and swimming in the huge outdoor
pool, and hanging out by the river.
And after a solid year together
we were wed in Place Capitole,
which made me quiver.

My mum, brothers and friends from
Barcelona came to our wedding,
and our French and Algerian pals too.
After our ceremony we had a small
gathering and later me and Abdenour
left to go on a cruise, just us two.

Abdenour is from Algeria,
his native tongue is Arabic and he
didn't speak any English back then.
We communicated in French
for the first few years then he asked
if I'd consider moving to Scotland again.

Loving the Rain

SCOTLAND

Abdenour loved living in Edinburgh,
he admired the city and even
loved the pouring rain!
He appreciated the public
transport to get around town
and that we had a local train.

He was happy he had found
a crew of Algerian buddies,
they'd hang out in the cafés.
The Arab men are known for this,
you often see them hanging
about there for days.

We toured the city's landmarks,
castles, cathedrals,
monuments and Dean village.
We visited the beaches, parks
and toured the city centre,
we put on a lot of mileage.

Abdenour struggled with the language
and with finding work at first,
he found this really tough.
But after a year or so he had
a thick Scottish accent,
and found a job sure enough.

He got a night-shift reception
job at a spiffy hotel, nestled
between the old and new town.
We stayed there for free and had
a view of the castle, plus I had spa
days there to help calm me down.

Exploring Careers in Edinburgh

I started my own business
teaching Spanish and French to kids
as an after school activity.
I soon had five employees and a
whole bunch of students, and I got
to use my skills and creativity.

Later on I went back to being
a student, I did a biological
science course at college.
I loved experimenting in the science
lab and was absorbed in learning
this intense new knowledge.

From there I went on to become
a student nurse, but after a year
I dropped out.
I knew by then this was not for me,
it was time to change gears
and find another route.

Before I left I had an incredible
moment with a patient who's
muscles were deteriorating.
He told me the use of his mind
and imagination still worked
and this for him was liberating.

He said that he was blessed to
have travelled the world and to
have eaten in fancy restaurants.
He could easily imagine himself
wherever he liked in his mind,
were he'd meet his needs and wants.

Throughout our time in Edinburgh,
I had a few other jobs on the side,
one with a home improvement store.
I did all the job roles. I stacked
shelves, did cashier, trained new
employees, team leader and more.

I also worked as a care worker,
caring for adults with disabilities,
with a few ladies, but mostly with one.
In the poem that follows
I share a piece I wrote
when my work with her was done.

A Pocket Full of Kisses

I cared for this wonderful
woman, for almost eight years.
One of the many gifts she shared
with me, was how to face my fears.

In no time she became a friend,
a sister, a real Angel of mine.
That amazing massive smile of hers
is just so powerfully divine.

I'd stay over at her place
and take care of her every need.
This closeness caused an internal
bonding that's raw and true, indeed.

Although her life was hard
at times, with epilepsy and all,
she was always rapidly back on
her feet, after every fall.

She taught me how to bounce back
quick and not stay down for long.
How to gather courage, smile again,
get my strength back and be strong.

We had so much fun together,
we'd sing and dance and play.
I'd always go home with a pocket full
of kisses, she'd kindly send my way.

As my journey continued, our time
of such physical closeness had to end.
But she will forever remain
my teacher, my sister, my friend.

Although it seems like
distance is keeping us apart,
wherever I may be I carry
her always in my heart.

Travelling with Abdenour

ALGERIA

We went to Algeria a good few times
to visit Abdenour's family, they all
speak French—this was handy.
We went to his brothers wedding,
the bride wore 7 dresses and I wore 4!
There was heaps of hand crafted candy.

Abdenour's family are from Algiers,
they live in a small two bedroom
flat, in a populated zone.
Seven of them lived there,
and it was common to go
to the mosque to snooze or be alone.

The building had nine floors and no lift,
people would raise their baskets up to
their windows using a rope.
I enjoyed shopping at the local markets
where I bought myself a nice tea set,
spices, pj's, and soap.

His parents and siblings welcomed
me with open arms, eager
to feed me food and show me around.
They cooked me a wide variety of
couscous dishes and borek, which I
ate with bread, and my smile was round.

We visited some sweet spots around
the city and went to what looked like
Algiers' version of the Eiffel Tower.
We travelled five hours south, to a
seaside town where more family members
lived and milled their own flour.

At the farmers market in town
you had your pick of live chickens,
which they'd slaughter there and then.
Headless chickens were running
about and they'd casually ask,
"would you prefer a cock or a hen?"

MOROCCO

Abdenour and I went to Morocco together,
where we spent eight hours on a camel
going across the desert.
We were on a mission to stay
overnight in a Bedouin's tent,
and upon arrival my ass really hurt.

They played drums, danced and cooked
tajine, and with the heat of the sun
they baked us bread in the hot sand.
There was nothing but emptiness
for miles and miles, it was incredible
how people lived on this land.

We visited a Berber village where
part of the movie Babel, with
Brad Pitt, was shot.
We saw mud houses and mud castles,
and we visited Jemaa el-Fnaa square,
a busy market spot.

Chapter 4
THE SEARCH FOR PERSIA

Finding my Family in Iran

As a wee girl I spoke
to my family in Iran,
in Farsi on the phone.
They'd send me food like gaas
and pistachios, my love for
both to them well known.

I never made it over
there to meet them,
before my dad passed.
In fact we lost touch
completely, long before
we moved to near Belfast.

In my early 20's my
fascination and desire for
my Iranian side began.
Eager to find my family,
explore the culture and
land—I needed a plan.

I was living in France
and there 'just happened to be'
a Persian festival in town.
I watched 3 movies in Farsi
in a row, with French subtitles,
this made me frown.

Back in Edinburgh, Scotland,
my search was stronger than ever.
I sought out all Iranians I could find
to help with this endeavour.

We exchanged English for Farsi
and they cooked me Iranian foods.
I called the Iranian and British embassies,
but had no luck with these dudes.

I visited the Persian rug shop often,
to get info from the vendor.
He said I could travel to Kish Island
with no visa—a possible idea of splendour.

I mentioned my search
to a new friend, who was
passionate about family trees.
And within 3 minutes of googling,
she discovered I had a sister,
who just might hold the other keys!

My mum and dad divorced
when I was 7 and dad
married an Iranian wife.
She was 7 months pregnant
when dad died, and she
brought the gift of a new life.

This new life was my baby
sister, who never got the
chance to meet our dad.
But I know that he helped
bring us together, for which
I am so grateful and glad.

I googled her name
and to my surprise,
she was living in the UK.
I typed her name into Facebook
and there she was—
"No-Way!"

Tears of joy
ran down my face,
as I typed a private note.
Our brother Dave, now
on board, was keen to
know what I'd wrote.

About 5 days later,
the perfect response arrived.
She wanted to meet us,
and our Iranian connection
got revived!

It was Time to Meet at Last

IRAN

The Iranian saga
was well on its way,
it was time to meet at last.
A journey that would begin
transforming the tragedy
from the past.

I was now 30 years old
and my long lost
grandmother was still alive.
The whole family
excitedly waiting for
me and Dave to arrive.

First we went to London
to meet our sister Orchid,
who was now 20 years old.
She's a wonderful singer,
songwriter, and a beautiful
being to behold.

She was raised in Oxford,
England, and we also visited
her sweet mum and sister there.
We ate Iranian food
and had many stories
to exchange and share.

The flight to Tehran was super
sweet, me and Dave magically
got upgraded to first class!
Just before landing an
announcement stated: all women
must cover their hair, body and ass.

We arrived at 4am,
and the whole family
were waiting at the airport.
They had come to greet
us, to meet us and
give us transport.

What a crazy, wonderful
moment this was for us all.
At one point my grandma
fell to her knees to crawl.

My uncle grabbed me
and hugged me,
and sobbed real hard.
It was as though we
had all been dealt an
almighty trump card.

I worried they wouldn't
care to meet us, but
this was not the case.
Grandma thanked God
the whole way home, where
there were photos of my face.

Our cousins translated that
our grandma had been
praying to meet us every day.
Now here she was meeting
her grandchildren, the children
of her son who had passed away.

Peach Cheeks

One of the first things we did
was visit my dad's grave.
His face was carved into the
gravestone, a surprise to me and Dave.

The whole trip was an emotional,
wild roller-coaster ride.
We travelled, we danced,
we sang, we laughed and we cried.

Everyone was so very glad
to see us, and would lovingly
grab and squeeze my cheeks.
According to my grandma my
cheeks were like peaches and
this squeezing went on for weeks!

They treated us like king and queen
and cooked us yummy food.
Luckily some family members spoke
English, or we'd have been screwed!

We have quite a big family there,
lots of aunts, uncles and cousins.
They seemed to just keep coming
with gifts for us by the dozens.

My uncle was rather touched
by the pocket watch
we brought him.
It reminded him of his last
encounter with my dad, where
he gave him his watch on a whim.

We toured Tehran, Qom, Mashhad,
Isfahan and Shiraz; we saw Persepolis
and many holy places.
We visited mosques and shrines
and us ladies had to wear chador—
you could only see our faces.

One day while visiting one of
these holy sites I lost my glasses,
down the 'hole in the ground' loo.
And since every women was
wearing black, I struggled to find
my aunt, and female cousins too!

Iran is such a different world
from the one I grew up in.
The Islamic law that is strictly enforced
makes most things a sin.

The land is super beautiful,
and the food is really delicious.
The people are really sweet,
it's just the laws that are kinda vicious.

Getting around in a
vehicle or walking about,
was often rather precarious.
I'd tuck myself under my grandma's
wing, eyes closed, to cross the road—
it was scary and hilarious.

We were only there
for about 17 days,
and we were in 3 car crashes!
A guy on his bike did get hurt,
but we were fortunately
not turned to ashes.

We also visited our sister
Orchid's family, who
welcomed us as their own.
They cooked us yummy food
and took us to places that we
had not yet been shown.

Our time there was short,
but it was such a blessed treat.
They all lived up to my name, 'Shereen',
in Farsi it means sweet.

At the airport my uncle
repeated history and gave
my brother our dad's watch.
An intense emotional moment
for Dave, it looked like
he needed a scotch.

We said our farewells
and off we went,
but we still keep in touch.
We talk to each other
on the phone and
love each other very much.

Me and grandma call each
other peach cheeks and my uncle
sings me songs about 'Shereen.'
Our connection and this
whole experience, continues
to make my heart beam.

Chapter 5
THE SEARCH FOR MOTHERHOOD

Trying to Get Pregnant

SCOTLAND

It started out rough
and grew worse and worse.
My worst nightmare would haunt me
as my shadow, my curse.

I wanted to hold my baby
in my arms so tight,
No pregnancy again and again
led to a brutal, persistent fight.

The sway from hope,
that this month was my time,
to the despair and grief,
and new huge mountain to climb.

Babies and pregnant women
everywhere to remind me of my lot.
The dreaded question "when are you having kids?"
made me feel I'd been shot.

After a bunch of medical visits,
surgery, and test after test,
the tireless journey got terribly dark.
I was so anxious and wholly depressed.

At first we got a misdiagnosis
about my husband's sperm's mobility.
Then we were diagnosed with having
unexplained infertility.

Later they said
my fallopian tubes were blocked;
I would need to consider another option.
No natural pregnancy
was possible, that I could try
IVF or adoption.

At this time
I would have done anything
to make this dream come true.
I saw motherhood
as my only way to end,
this purposeless future point of view.

It was nearly my turn;
I had been on the waiting list
for IVF for almost three years.
Then five months before my turn,
my eight year relationship ended
with my spouse from Algiers...

Defeatism Evoked a Glimpse of Paradise

Weeks before our breakup,
I had an intense experience
whilst lying on the floor.
My whole body wept
as I 'shed a skin' and
witnessed my being soar.

Then without warning,
everything started
to drop away.
Divine interventions
were taking place and
I couldn't make anything stay.

My marriage was over
and my chance to meet
my children gone.
My current religious beliefs
had left and with them
some friends I leaned upon.

In a state of defeatism,
where I felt like
I had nothing else to lose,
in a meditative state,
I fell into a deep surrender,
and landed on a peaceful cruise.

Nowhere to go,
nothing to need or want,
nothing to think about.
An almighty moment
of freedom where I was
completely blissed out.

A few days later, however,
my mind structures
re-gained their hold.
And I dreamed
of a new life and new lover,
and the baby we'd hold.

The Grassmarket Community Project

In order to help myself
recover from the grief
and loss I had been enduring,
I joined the Grassmarket
Community Project.
And found it truly helpful and alluring.

It's a project set up to help people
going through transitions,
reconnnecting disengaged folk.
Here I unearthed my creative talents,
and met people recovering from
all sorts of stuff, i.e. smoking coke.

They had creative writing workshops,
and I participated in a zine making class—
they were enlightening and fun.
I tried painting and woodworking,
and making herbal medicines,
I tried them all out one by one.

Getting involved in this
wonderful project, enabled me
to slowly re-open my heart.
It made me want to find ways
to heal and fulfil my dreams,
and turn my life into a work of art.

I got a new flatmate from India
who brought love, joy
and spice back into my space.
We had fun going out on the
town together and watching movies,
I loved her cute wee face.

By this stage in my life
I had been sober for nearly seven years,
but I now felt the need to go wild.
I needed relief and some high level fun,
I needed to break free,
and to become a flower child.

Meeting Angel Gabriel

Part 1 - Luscious Locks

The Bongo Club was bouncing,
I danced the night away.
The reggae music was real sweet,
it made me move and sway.

After the dance was over,
I left the club on a high.
I bobbed down the alley,
and there he was—MY GUY!

He was hanging by the dumpster,
looking all scruffy and tall.
Puppy dog eyes, sweet cheeks,
luscious locks and all.

My bus was not due
for another hour or two,
I asked if he fancied hanging
out till my bus came through.

He said yes and we wandered
up the street to the local park—
sat on a bench, huddled close,
to keep warm in the dark.

He shared his stories about
busking and hitch hiking.
I was hooked and found
him rather wise and striking.

There was something about him
right from the start.
Like our souls had met before,
our meeting a work of art.

As time went by
and the cold wind blew,
our hearts and lips grew closer,
when onto his knee I flew.

He wrapped one arm around me
and placed the other on my knee,
then in for the kiss he went,
for a prolonged moment of glee.

As the night came to an end
and it was time to say goodbye,
we knew that from this moment forth
our love would grow and never die.

Part 2 - The Orange Peel

He wanted to exchange contact
details, so we could meet again.
"I'd like to give you my email so we
can arrange the next where-n-when."

But neither of us had phones
or pen or paper at hand.
So he got out his caveman skills
and sought out answers from the land.

As he looked around
the solution became clear;
there was a prime orange peel
and a stone to engrave with near.

He handed me the orange peel
with hope in his eyes,
and we hugged it out
and said our goodbyes.

After a day or so
I decided it was time to write.
But by then the orange peel had shrivelled
and there was no email in sight!

I tried to make it out
and sent emails to what I thought it may be.
They all bounced back
and with sadness I thought, "Not meant to be."

Two months later I got a surprise in my inbox,
"Picnic?"
He had found me, how did he do that?
this Mr Slick.

It turns out I'd mentioned our meeting
to a buddy back when,
who happened to know his father
and shared of our meeting just then.

And here we were reunited again,
it was time to dance and blend.
Journeying onward together
as lovers—my new best friend.

Tuscany and the Robber in Rome

ITALY

Not long after I met Gabriel
I took myself off to Italy for a month,
to do a workaway.
I stayed with a family
in this gorgeous spot, surrounded by
sunflower fields in Tuscany.

I took care of their young kids,
they practiced English,
and I did some farming.
The dad was a yoga teacher,
who also taught laughing yoga,
and was rather charming.

As luck would have it,
a friend of theirs,
a shaman from Peru, came to stay.
He came to do an ayahuasca ceremony,
that would take place
the very next day.

They asked if I wanted to join them,
but I had no idea what this was,
or what to expect.
I trusted the family
and agreed. I felt guided,
had faith and respect.

Ayahuasca is a powerful brew,
a spiritual drug, that claims
to open your mind and heal trauma.
It has hallucinogenic properties,
and can give you access to inner knowledge,
as well as deal with drama.

This was the most intense experience
I've ever had,
it truly was like dying and being reborn.
I felt like I gave birth to myself,
a surge of energy made my mind expand,
and it helped me mourn.

Everyone in the room was vomiting
into their buckets, I was sweating
like a pig and couldn't stop crying.
The shaman sang songs and played music,
that I found painful and irritating at first,
but it later became truly gratifying.

The ayahuasca trip lasted about 6 hours
and I cried for at least 3 hours straight—
I sat with all my pain.

Soon I shifted into a blissful state
and could hear the music with my heart,
I'd hopped upon a brand new train.

Soon after the ayahusaca deep dive,
it was time to say farewell
and head towards the big city.
I jumped on a train and headed south,
were I wrote my first rhyming poem,
it was truly profound and pretty.

I stayed in a hostel for a week in Rome,
I visited cathedrals and cat castles.
I munched on gelato.
Three robbers who considered robbing me,
instead gave me what they'd stolen that day,
I thought I'd won the lotto.

Dreaming New Dreams with Gabriel

We will build our yurt,
the hub of our home.
The seed of our sanctuary
in which we shall roam.

In finding the perfect
spot to plant,
we will grow and grow
and never say can't.

We will witness sunsets
and dance under the moon.
Reconnect with the seasons
and transform in June.

We will create,
inspire and heal.
And bring awareness
to all that's real.

Flow with life through
its storms and seas.
Into its tranquillity,
blessed with its breeze.

Backpacking Travels with Gabriel

PORTUGAL/UK

We travelled the UK, touring
Scotland, England, Ireland and Wales.
We visited family, we camped
and explored new zones and new trails.

We visited the peak district,
wild camping in a green field
at the bottom of a hill.
In the morning our tent was surrounded
by sheep, staring as though a spaceship had landed,
their voices echoing and shrill.

We went on a backpacking holiday
to Portugal—to Lisbon and Lagos.
We wild camped and stayed in Airbnb's,
and ate pasta with no sauce.

Our Airbnb in Lisbon was near
a gorgeous view point,
with glorious sunsets.
Our host hooked us up and
suggested we visit Lagos.
We did and have no regrets.

Lagos was stunning, the beach front
is absolutely wonderful,
it has such epic cliffs.
There is a walled old town,
very near the beach,
the whole zone full of gifts.

One day on the beach,
a guy who referred to himself
as 'Mikey Angel' appeared.
He invited us to
a 'rainbow gathering,'
which turned out to be really weird.

On the way there we got
hitch hiked at the bus station,
by a family in their hippy van.
On arrival we got hugged down
by naked bodies and there was
this naked, crazy old man.

At first we thought his yelling
and shaking and behaviour was
just part of the rainbow thing.
But apparently not, he was
wrestled to the ground, just before
our meal where we'd circle and sing.

Back in Edinburgh, my flat mate
from India went home
and Gabriel moved in with me.
My brother Sean joined us for a bit
and we got two bunnies,
who loved to poo and pee.

Happy's Hostel by the Ganges

INDIA

Gabriel, my new found
love in my life, brought
joy and light to my heart.
This helped me to
dream new dreams—
a new chapter did start.

However, the pain and dream
around having children
was still super strong.
But the thought of IVF
or the route of adoption
both for me now felt wrong.

Both options felt invasive,
one on my body and the other
on my personal space.
And both myself and Gabriel
hoped there was another way
we could experience this grace.

I had always wanted to go
to India, and I hoped that
there maybe I'd find a cure.
Plus the thought of doing
a Yoga Teacher Training Course,
was a bonus reason to go, for sure.

I hoped that I would find a
way to heal my body and
be able to naturally conceive.
But by now, after over
five years of trying, this
was really hard to believe.

I made a deal with myself,
that I would find a cure,
or find a way to let this go.
And so off I went to Rishikesh,
India, were I knew
I was bound to grow.

India is the most colourful,
spicy, smelly, loud, visually
full on, sensory place I know.
And even after a hectic 8 hour
taxi ride to my zone by the Ganges,
I felt myself begin to glow.

I stayed in Happy's hostel
with Ganesh and Krishna,
so I felt well looked after by the gods.
The yoga classes were a little trek away,
which meant sneaking by monkeys,
who'd often hang out in squads.

My fellow classmates
and my teachers,
were all so incredibly awesome.
The whole experience of being
there was helping my
heart to blossom.

The Yoga Teacher Training
was hardcore, from 6am to 8pm
of solid classes.
With some breaks of course,
to chill by the Ganges
and wear my sunglasses.

We did Vinyasa and Hatha Yoga,
Yoga Therapy, Theory,
Pranayama and Meditation.

Anatomy and Physiology,
Chanting and Philosophy—
all brought a feeling of elation.

On the weekends
we went rafting down the Ganges,
and took a trip to visit a temple.
I enjoyed the colourful, mystical shops,
restaurants and tuk-tuk rides,
that were neither smooth nor gentle.

Our whole class got invited
to one of the teacher's weddings,
and I got to wear some Indian attire.
And we were there for Holi,
were we threw coloured powder on
each other, and saw a tall bonfire.

We graduated on 4/20,
with some fun cannabis
celebrations by the river.
I met with a lady I hoped
could help me heal,
"would she be able to deliver?"

She was a naturopathic doctor,
who gave me some tips
and tricks to try out.
I also felt the good food
and exercise I was getting
would help no doubt.

I spent my final week
attending a dance class and
chilling by the Ganges river.
I had the most amazing time
there, and I left India
on the highest high ever.

From the Highest High to the Lowest Low

SCOTLAND

Back in Edinburgh,
I was reunited with Gabriel,
happy and excited about our future together.
I covered a few yoga classes
at the chaplaincy and did lots of Tai Chi,
I felt as light as a feather.

However, after some time we decided
to move into a room above a church,
near Gabriel's parents place.
This is where the realization
that I'd never meet my babies hit,
the time had come to drop the chase.

I sank into the deepest grief
that made my back hurt real
bad, I could hardly even walk.
I thought the roller coaster ride
of trying to conceive was hard,
but this was harder, I was frozen with shock.

This room was the perfect sanctuary
for me to move through this tough experience,
it was the perfect place for me to be.
The church garden, the canal and woods near by—
were my go-to places, where I could
catch a breath and drink tea.

Me and Gabriel had turned the garage
into a woodworking zone,
where we began to make wooden treasures.
This creative endeavour helped
me to receive at least a little
sun ray, providing much needed pleasures.

The Funeral and Letter to my Unborn Children

Feeling forced to accept
that my dream of
motherhood was dead,
I felt drawn to paint
with my period blood
and wrote this letter that said:

To my unborn children,

With a broken heart
and years of tears,
flames of pure love
melt away my fears.

Fly dear little
ones, be free.
You will always be
an integral part of me.

Like a beautiful flower
is how I'll remain.
Free from the torment
and from intense pain.

My roots are stronger
and my leaves more green.
I have a blossoming heart,
that has touched the unseen.

I know your playfulness,
fearlessness and curiosity
will guide my ways.
And your eagerness to learn
and state of wonderment
will forever fill my days.

Thank you. I will always love you... Mum xoxoxoxoxox

I planted a plant
and had a little ceremony
with my guy.
Later I burned the painting
and poem with a dear friend,
to say goodbye.

Although these gestures
and movements were
helping me heal,
I didn't know how to digest this,
I did not want
this to be real.

I struggled to accept it;
I still secretly hoped
a natural pregnancy would come.
I was unable to consider a future
with no children of mine
to call me mum.

And the pattern of bouncing
from 'hope to despair'
was still fully there.
I surrendered into being
swallowed by grief,
it made me more Aware.

Chapter 6
THE SEARCH FOR HEALING, PEACE AND PURPOSE

Kefah

The pain and reality
of my losses were in full swing,
demanding my attention.
I needed some sort
of professional support,
to help me release the tension.

This time, instead of going
to a doctor to help me
with my mood and pain,
I sought out a spiritual healer
and she helped me
over and over again.

Kefah is a counsellor
and shaman, and she took me
on some powerful healing trips.
I discovered my inner sanctuary
and met my spirit guides
and got some badass tips.

She helped me re-connect
with my soul and get
my feet back on the ground.
I participated in her deep
intensive courses, these were
truly great and profound.

I met some wonderful spiritual
warriors who also had come to
regain peace and heal.
This was not an easy ride,
it meant we all had to allow
ourselves to truly feel.

We went deep into healing
the pain of our past, and we
faced our present struggles.
We were given tools and practices
that helped move us through them
and feel our spirits' cuddles.

I Needed a Change of Scenery

Myself and Gabriel had been
dreaming over the years of some
day moving to a sunnier spot.
We considered Italy, Spain, France
and the US, I needed
somewhere new, nice and hot.

I made an effort to focus on this
dream, make some big decisions,
and get things moving.
Brexit helped us choose the US,
though at first mum was disapproving.

Because Gabriel's mum is from
New York and he's a US citizen,
there was a way this could work.
During our immigration process
Trump banned all Iranians,
I thought "oh shit, what a jerk!"

We allowed ourselves to dream,
"let's get married and find a place
where we can grow our own food."
We needed a new beginning, a new
adventure, more peace, more fun—
this we truly understood.

Gabriel's mum, now on board
with our idea, offered him a job
in her business in their old town.
In fact she needed him there ASAP,
so off he went, and we kept our fingers crossed,
the visa would be given to me hands down.

I wrote the poem that follows
during this time in waiting,
while he was in the USA, me in the UK.
Months had passed and no word on my visa,
but a heron came to say,
"be patient and know all will be OK."

Fuck the Borders

Desiring to be on the
other side of the ocean,
to be with my lover
and put our dreams into motion.

The borders and immigration laws
make this real hard.
Fill out a million forms
and spend with that bank card.

Even after all the forms, medical tests
and money spent,
your fate is in an 'officials' hands,
you need their consent!

I am patiently waiting
for the day to arrive,
to decide whether or not
the immigration officer should survive.

Powerlessness creeps in,
from time to time.
No freedom of movement,
oh what a crime!

I trust that the universe
is on my side.
I choose to relax, stay present
and enjoy the ride.

First Month in Wisconsin

USA

*I wrote this poem one month in
to my move to the USA.
It sure was an intense beginning,
I must say.*

The sun has been blazing,
the swim spots amazing.

The fireflies are epic,
they light up the night.
There are many creatures
about that bite.

The people have been friendly,
generous and kind.
The land is stunning here,
there are many new spots to find.

We first lived in our home,
The Bell Tent.
But a flood came
and off some of
our possessions went.

We stayed in a hotel
for a week, with
other flood refugees.
A friend offered
a place to stay,
to which we said, yes please!

We are now in a beautiful valley,
living life off grid.
Solar panels, an outhouse,
tub of water with a lid.

Miles away from any town,
at first we just had bikes.
Now we've got
ourselves a badass truck,
and we're off on many hikes.

Everything is huge here
and the roads are
long and wide.
There are rolling hills
and trees, on
each and every side.

There are many
lovely lakes, rivers
and streams.
Canoeing and kayaking
are the things to do,
it seems.

We are soon to move
into our new
wee house in town.
To settle before winter,
before the leaves
have dropped down.

It's a lovely wee bungalow,
near the local park.
Gonna get ourselves a wood stove,
for when it's cold and dark.

I've been doing
odd jobs here and there.
Meeting many new creatures,
luckily not yet a bear.

The Wedding Party

The day of the party
was extra great.
I managed to release the struggles
and connect with my mate.

Leading up to the party
was mega intense.
Strong emotions and deadlines,
energies so dense.

Despite the chaos,
confusion and stress,
what an amazing day
it was nonetheless.

There was sunlight by day
and moonlight by night.
And it felt rather special
to be dressed in white.

The bell tent was back,
a zone to hang out in and rest.
Everything about the party
made me feel grateful and blessed.

Great friends helped
make our visions come true.
A beautiful spot, a sound system,
a compost loo.

There was live music,
dancing and a fire too.
Lawn games, great food,
a lovely intimate crew.

Flowers, bunting
and lighting galore.
Shelter and a trough hot tub.
Who could ask for more?

My Multimedia Masta

It turns out Gabriel is
a multimedia masta,
who loves to drink tea
and eat pizza and pasta.

He makes badass tunez
and takes sweet photos,
as well as playing ukulele
in the streets and meadows.

He's a digital designer,
designing websites and books,
he makes videos, is a gardener
and carpenter, and he cooks!

Mostly we live in harmony
and make a good team.
But like every other couple,
we sometimes make each other scream.

In a poem from him to me he wrote;
I was sweeter than cream,
more supreme, than any queen,
his dearest sweet Shereen.

To listen to Gabriel's badass beats visit:
www.kaveman-tunez.bandcamp.com

Grateful

Grateful for our decision
to move across the Ocean.
Grateful for our courage
to put our dreams in motion.

Grateful for our strength,
that meets challenges along the way.
Grateful for the lessons learned,
each and every day.

Grateful for our house, a base
where we can ground and grow.
Grateful for the intense seasons,
for the blazing sun and snow.

Grateful for our adventures,
our inner and outer explorations.
Grateful for the tools, creative
expression and for all the celebrations.

We Moved to Town

We moved to a gorgeous
little town in the Midwest.
People's yards are stunning here,
I'm still super impressed.

It's abundant with beauty,
and filled with generous souls.
It's a place that's conducive
to people achieving their goals.

For the first years
I was still grieving.
At the same time, trying to
open myself up to receiving.

My world was both
super dark and yet,
also super bright.
The blue sky was
informing me, everything
was gonna be alright.

I got a job with a
wonderful local family,
who make maple syrup to sell.
The job has been meditative,
and has given me a sacred
cave-like place to dwell.

I began attending gatherings
and going to events
to meet new folks.
We gather, sing and
dance together and
tell each other jokes.

There are wise teachers all
around, at One Spirit,
many wise old souls.
And at the school,
where I care for young kids,
they too are playing their roles.

The community is full of artists,
musicians and healers,
doing their thing.
And the beautiful nature
has much to say and teach,
I hear it laugh and sing.

The almighty Mississippi river
is only a 30 minute drive away.
There are wonderful parks, lakes and trails,
were I can go and play.

Amish folk live in the area,
they get around
via horse and cart.
They sell veggies at the
farmers market and
also sell their art.

The weather and seasons
are intense here, it gets
both boiling and freezing.
The sun shines most of the
year regardless of the season,
and I find this extremely pleasing.

An Unexpected Discovery

When we first moved
into our little house,
it was creepy.
It was dingy and full of
cockroaches, and I found
it really hard to get sleepy.

While I battled with childlessness
on the inside, I also battled
with cockroaches on the outside.
I soon discovered that our struggles
are our teachers and when we learn
the lessons they move aside.

Cockroaches only come out in the
dark, they run from the light,
and they are tough as boots.
If we want to truly heal and
move on, we must do what
we can to get to the roots.

I began inquiring into my reasons
for wanting children and why
this hurt so much.
Down through the layers,
where under the surface there
are gems to see and touch.

A mystical encounter arose,
that involved the discovery
of my new house's 'tubes being blocked.'
An appointment to unblock them,
and another to possibly unblock mine
on the same day knocked!

An appointment for an
alternative method, Mayan
massage, and I couldn't resist.
It didn't get me pregnant,
but led me to a discovery
that up until then did not exist.

On this day it became clear
to me that only part of me
wanted to raise 'my own' child.
And to my surprise there was
another part that didn't and
I took a deep breath and smiled.

I was both sad that I'd never get to
hold my child's hands or see their
smiles and give them kisses and cuddles,
and also glad that I'd never
have to witness their suffering, their
pain, their death, and their struggles.

I'm sadly childless
AND gratefully childfree,
I'm willing to make space for both.
In opening up
to accommodate each,
came new opportunities for growth.

I soon met an angel who brought me
the possibility to teach English
in an orphanage in Thailand.
My prayer to serve motherless children
had been heard and I was off
to lend my heart-n-hand.

Our house underwent
a complete transformation,
the cockroaches vanished.
And our house got
brighter and felt lighter,
as the darkness banished.

Super Transformational

THAILAND

My trip to Thailand was a
huge step in my healing—
I can finally be around kids again!
I notice too, I can admire the beauty
of pregnant women and babies
and feel way more zen.

Before embarking on this journey,
I made the intention
to give and receive love.
And from the moment
I arrived in Bangkok, I was swept up
and carried by a heavenly dove.

I spent the first week or so teaching
English in the kindergarten school
in Klong Toey slum.
I felt super cared for by the
Duang Prateep Foundation,
who made me feel truly welcome.

The slum kids were incredibly sweet,
and their English was pretty impressive.
They had some cool dance moves
and their wee faces were so expressive.

Then I was transported
to the New Life Project
in Kanchanaburi, 135km away.
To this wondrous place in nature,
where about 60 kids,
between ages 5 and 20 stay.

Kru Prateep, the Slum Angel,
set this project in motion
with the support of her team.
And helped by donations
from around the globe,
she is fulfilling her dream.

This particular project serves
children who have been orphaned,
left homeless or abused.
It gives them the space they need
to recover from being physically
and emotionally bruised.

The zone provides lots of love,
food, shelter and a bus
to take the kids to school.
They can learn to bake,
cut hair and grow food
and they go on outings to the local pool.

The kids were super adorable
and I was so in Love
with all their cute wee faces.
When not on teacher duty,
I was playing with them
and giving them warm embraces.

To get an inside view of Klong Toey Slum in Bangkok and the epic works of the Duang Prateep Foundation search 'shereen's journey teaching english in thailand' on Youtube.

Childless Mother Meets Motherless Children

This poem was born from our meeting,
which truly was a delightful greeting.

At last I now know
a huge part of why I am here.
To find you, play with you,
love you and hold you, oh so dear.

To kiss your cheeks, hug you,
hear you, and hold your hand.
To teach you and encourage you
to grow and expand.

To bring opportunities
and knowledge to your door.
Be an inspiration to you
and boost your desires to explore.

To help you to see the dreams
and truths that lie deep
within your soul.
So you can go forth,
free from fear, and from
that arduous need to control.

Those Babyless Blues, No Longer our Daily News

Not at the forefront of our day,
stealing our joy away.

New things have our attention,
and we have a deeper comprehension.

About life and its ways,
and the peace that stays.

Now we go forth born anew.
No longer feeling so goddamn blue.

Childfull, Childfree AND Free to Mother Many

My childlessness gives me
the gift of a childfree lifestyle,
and the freedom to mother many.
I have personally learned
a lot from women who choose
to be childfree and don't want any.

I am endlessly pregnant
with possibilities and ideas,
and I take care of my own inner child.
I am endlessly giving birth
to miracles as my heart
becomes ever more reconciled.

I have found many ways
to express my motherly tendencies—
to love, nurture, care, raise and teach.
And the dance of childless and
childfree has a new horizon,
now 'childfull and childfree' is in reach.

I have an ultra adorable kitty cat,
Sage, who is super friendly,
cuddly and fluffy.
I have an incredibly wonderful man,
who is super talented,
cuddly and scruffy.

I honour the childless me, I hold her
when she's sad and I let the childfree
me be wild and creative.
Both parts work together to create
a life I love living, where I can be
of service and be innovative.

I recently created
The Flowerhood Project,
which is still in its early stages.
A place where I share tools and
practices, for those ready to write
their own futures pages.

I love the time freedom
I have to make art, play, write,
go on road trips and travel about.
I'm loving the opportunity
to learn to grow my own food
and try new things, and just chill out.

Novice Gardener

Our yard was once a blank
canvas covered in snow.
We planted seeds indoors
and wondered if they'd grow.

After germination the
seedlings did appear.
Whether they'd grow to food
was still dubious and unclear....

After months inside
given love and light,
the gradual move to the outdoors
seemed ripe and right.

We prepared our spiral beds
all ready for our seedlings
and new seeds.
Not long after being
in the ground, commenced
the battle with the weeds.

At first the seedlings
were small and the weeds
would stunt their growth.
Thus watering and
removing weeds became
the main tasks for us both.

To our surprise, our garden
is now in full bloom.
Every patch of the spiral is full,
there is no more room.

We have tomatoes, zucchini, squash,
fennel, potatoes, ground cherries,
chard and leeks.
We have onions, peppers, lettuce
and kale. Some are ready now
others in just a few weeks.

We have a crew of herbs:
basil, parsley, rosemary, sage,
oregano and thyme.
We have berry shrubs,
plum and cherry trees,
and cool green beans that climb.

We have medicinal herbs
such as valerian, calendula,
comfrey, chamomile and lemon balm.
These are particularly helpful
for insomnia, inflammation,
healing wounds and keeping calm.

Our pharmacy of organic food
and medicinal herbs
is right outside our back door.
Here's to health, saving money
and fewer visits to
the doctor and store.

Watch the garden unfold, search 'shereen baird the garden comes alive' on Youtube.

Chapter 7
THE SEARCH FOR ANSWERS TO THE BIG QUESTIONS

Looking for Answers in Religions

My mum was brought up Catholic,
my dad was brought up Muslim,
both in pretty strict ways.
They made the choice to not impose
any religion onto us, we were free to
choose who and what to praise.

At 16 years old I converted to
Christianity and later tried on atheism,
none of which quenched my thirst.
I explored Hinduism, Buddhism, Taoism and others,
as I was driven by a search for truth,
my blessing and my curse.

My first husband was a practicing Muslim
and his outlook on life fascinated me,
I loved how he handled things.
His presence and support got me off
mood-meds and to never need
them again, this gave me new wings.

I met a French girl who had
converted to Islam and she convinced me
to go to the mosque with her one day.
Taken aback that my soul wanted me
to immerse myself in this new religion,
I soon began to pray.

Abdenour was surprised when I came home
and told him I had taken the Shahada,
the declaration of faith to enter Islam.
I was soon praying 5 times a day,
participating in Ramadan, fasting
and greeting with the word 'Salam.'

Praying at the mosque was
an exhilarating experience for me and
I was blessed to meet amazing girls.
I learned the Arabic alphabet and
how to recite verses from the Quran.
I unearthed so many pearls.

I was a devout Muslim for almost 4 years.
I even wore a headscarf
and fully covered up for almost one year.
One day while on a yoga retreat,
I had a shift occur inside that was guiding me out,
this vision was real clear.

Islam was a necessary stepping stone for me,
but it was clear it was time to break out
of what had become a box.
And this is when I began to turn inward
for answers instead, and I noticed
that the God within me talks.

Finding Tools and Practices that Work for Me

I first discovered yoga
in Barcelona, Spain.
Straight up it enhanced my joy
and reduced and eased my pain.

I've tried the many styles,
to explore what works for me,
what brings me balance,
strength, focus and flexibility.

I've had the privilege to
learn and practice with
many great teachers.
They're still my mentors,
so too are the
plants and creatures.

Stepping onto my mat
each and every day,
I reconnect and center,
and let stillness light the way.

Off the mat I see the signs
and hear nature speak.
My faith, trust and confidence grows
and I feel less and less weak.

I not only practice yoga,
I also enjoy chi-gong and tai-chi.
I take from the buffet of life
the practices that benefit me.

Understanding the Mystery of Time

I was 7, with my dad in his car,
and we stopped at the petrol
station to get some gas.
I saw a stuffed toy I really wanted,
he said "no," and I screamed
and nearly broke the glass.

"I want that teddy" I sobbed and
screamed, I was adamant I get
this toy, and finally he got it for me.
This might sound like a spoiled brat
having a tantrum, but wee me knew—
I needed this in the future to help set me free.

This stuffed toy of a mother pig, holding
her baby pig, has been a helpful companion
on my journey to motherhood my way.
I brought her to the funeral and to all
the ceremonies I held for my children,
it's now on my altar today.

Miss piggy is so charged with both
positive and negative energy for me—
a reminder of death and childlessness.
Yet also a symbol of birth, aliveness,
motherhood, Love, my children, my dad,
and the taste of our timelessness.

Thanks to this whole journey,
I am more able to appreciate the gifts
of broken dreams, and the gain in every loss.
I have more compassion for my
fellow humans, and can take charge
of my life—I'm my own boss.

Trying to Understand the Dark Cloud

Not sure where it comes from,
or why it's here.
Not sure I can continue onward,
maybe death is near.

Drained of life,
plagued with sorrow,
the dark cloud comes and goes,
I wonder will it be gone tomorrow?

So much to live for,
so many people who care.
My family, my friends,
my handsome teddy bear.

Even sad moments never last,
they are sure to go.
The light always shines again,
this I know.

Looking for Guidance and Courage

It's ok not to know,
relax and let your light grow.

The power in you
will lead the way.
Just take baby steps
every day.

Release, have faith,
feel peace and joy.
Notice the beauty,
breathe and enjoy.

THE SEARCH FOR ANSWERS TO THE BIG QUESTIONS

You have much to teach,
create and share.
Express your love,
and show you care.

Sing and dance,
release pain and fear.
Do what you love,
and let money appear.

Have the courage
to step out,
and try your best.
Just focus on what
matters now,
and leave the rest.

You can do this,
support and guidance
are by your side.
Your contribution
will impact others,
far and wide.

Trust yourself
to do your thing.
You'll be surprised
at what you'll bring.

Now off you go,
dear one.
The journey's all yours,
have fun!

The Keys to Heal Past and Present Pain

Tired and weary,
struggling to sleep,
maybe I should consider
counting some sheep.

Or maybe the night
has something to share.
It could be a warning,
an alert to beware.

Tonight is day three
of restless snooze.
And this morning I dreamt
I drank too much booze.

Why am I anxious,
why am I stressed?
I want morning already,
I want to get dressed.

My nurturing
parent self is near,
informing me that
I have nothing to fear.

I am here with you,
and I really do care.
You're held snug,
my sweet teddy bear.

My child self feels
more at ease,
now curious and opened,
I am presented with keys.

My adult self now
comes into play,
with missions to accomplish
before the new day.

What are these keys for,
and why are there loads?
Some to open old wounds,
others lead to new roads.

I have the keys
to heal the past,
make peace with the present,
and feel free at last.

Be patient, as the opportunity
to use each key will come.
Stay calm and opened,
do not fear and go numb.

Remember you're held,
and that everything is alright,
and remember the secrets,
that have been shared tonight.

Now close your eyes,
and sleep dear child.
Your future is a blank canvas,
and you're free to go wild.

Looking for my Deceased Relatives

I centered myself in joy and asked,
"Dad, if you're there let me know"
and was guided to a song, *Children Children* by Macka B.
The lyrics go "never forget how great you are, Yes papa,
never underrate this, shall we celebrate this"—
I know he's here with me.

On the one hand, loss, death and change
are inevitable for us all. And on the other,
we are unmoved and eternal.
This means our 'dead' relatives and dreams
are fully alive, and we can be with them
whenever we want—life IS loving and maternal.

Joy is the direction to follow,
its also the path, and the destination too,
and the destination is right here NOW.
We can cultivate joy anytime,
because WE ARE JOY, and here everything
we could ever want is ours and we know how.

We know how to be with our relatives
or dreams, in other planes of existence,
where they are available.
We know who we are at our core,
temporal, eternal,
limitless and scalable.

Life Beyond Death

What happens to us when we die?
This is a question I've often pondered.
Moving through life aimlessly,
with no direction I've often wandered.

I've heard what religions say about life
after death and the journey of the soul.
I've experienced at times my life feeling
incomplete and other times already whole.

Those who have had near death experiences
teach us about the light that awaits.
I've achieved many 'out of this world'
experiences when in trance-like states.

Then there are those who claim to be
able to communicate with or see the dead.
I've seen signs from deceased loved ones,
some would say I've been misled.

Personally I don't see death as an
ending or something we need to fear.
I would love my friends and family
to send me off with good cheer.

Finding the Middle Ground

I notice that I've swung
to the extreme sides of
the pendulum, on a myriad of subjects.
And that both extreme experiences
were necessary for my journey,
which has been rather complex.

From hanging out topless
with nudists downtown, to being
completely covered from head to toe.
From eating anything, to eating vegan.
From extreme emotions that
either took me very high or very low.

From being a complete non participant
in a certain religion,
to fully trying this is on as my truth.
From full out smoking weed everyday,
to complete sobriety—extremes have been
teaching me from my youth.

Teaching me, that most of the time
the middle ground is best, but that
sometimes it's necessary that we sway.
Life continues to teach me that
my choices matter, and by knowing extremes,
I can better decide what's best each day.

Following and Trusting the Signs

Life continuously throws us
answers in the form of
signs and synchronicities.
This helps us discern what to do,
or where to go next, and shows
us our distinct abilities.

I've been shown so many
signs along the way,
which I've mostly followed.
That's why I'm where I am today.

For instance...

My break up with my first husband
led to the remembrance of an ex,
we called each other Bongo.
This led to a Bob Marley reggae
party at the Bongo Club, where I
met my new guy from near Chicago.

My ex husband wrote me a letter
with 'don't worry be happy'
written at the end.
The first song this new guy sang to
me was 'don't worry be happy',
and he became my new boyfriend!

Understanding My Purpose Progression

My purpose as a little kid
To play, explore, discover and learn,
from a place of awe and wonderment.
To fit in, comply, conform and learn,
to survive in a harsh environment.

My purpose as a teenager and young adult
To rebel, party and break the rules,
and let myself go wild.
To go out there on my own, travelling—
no longer a dependent child.

My purpose as a young maturing adult (early 20s)
To meet new people and try new things,
and learn how to make a living.
To seek out love, home, meaning and truth,
and learn to be forgiving.

My purpose as a maturing adult (20's and 30's)
To be directed to the inner world
by all the trauma, tragedy and pain.
To heal the wounds, reconnect with Life,
and learn to re-program my brain.

My purpose as a maturing adult (30's and 40's)
To uncover the hidden talents,
that are wrapped up in all the shadows.
To transform over and over again,
and be free to serve, create and compose.

Looking Out at the World for Answers

What do you see?
Look!
What do you see?
The joining of hearts,
united as we.

The stars and the moon,
the sun and the rain.
The happiness, the sadness,
the joy and the pain.

The plants and the trees.
The land, sky and seas.
The honey, wine, oil and cheese.

The gift of the senses—
smell, sound, taste, sight.
The tender touch and strength
to hold on tight.

The seasons,
the night and the day.
All of which come bearing guidance,
to show us the way.

Who am I? Is there a purpose?
Why am I here?
Wisdom shines its light,
often when pain is near.

I wish it were simple,
that someone or something
would wave a magic wand.
Revealing the inner knowledge,
the secrets of the self,
the universe and beyond.

Turning Inward to Find the Answers

Now look closer,
look from the heart.
What do you see?

I see the centre,
my centre.
The centre where I
must enter.

Into the place where
inner knowledge can be found.
Where the senses go beyond
hearing, sight, taste, smell and sound.

Where I can heal
and transform.
Where again and again,
I can be re-born.

Where the rain may pour
or the sun may shine,
where the deeper understanding
of the experience is mine.

Where I can re-visit
and shake hands with the past.
And give thanks for the wisdom given,
which is sure to last.

Where I can acknowledge
the beauty in the pain.
Where there is wisdom
and sacred knowledge to gain.

Where my state of
consciousness can shift.
Where into other
dimensions I can drift.

Where the seeing of cycles,
the circle of life is clear.
Where I can hold myself
and all beings dear.

Where a vital tool that guides
are my breaths.
Where I can experience
mini births and mini deaths.

Where I can give up the attachments
and all the confusion.
Where I can fly to that place
that's beyond all illusion.

Where energies transform
replacing the old,
opening gateways to pathways
paved with gold.

Where I can nurture
my inner child.
Where new desires
I must follow run wild.

Where I can feel the eternal life force
move through me,
liberating my fears,
thus setting me free.

Where now, the present moment,
is all that exists.
Where the worries of the past and future
no longer persist.

Where I know that everything is
and will be fine.
Where everything I could ever want or need
is already mine.

Where there is no need to climb or struggle,
no big wall.
Where I can appreciate life and
give thanks for all.

Chapter 8
LIFE'S WISDOM
AND WHAT I'VE LEARNED

The Wisdom of the Weeds

The garden whispers words of wisdom;
it's an ultimate reflection of life.
It teaches of a deeper Love,
beyond that of man and wife.

It has taught me that I AM a student gardener,
with a fistful of seeds at hand.
A gardener of the heart and mind,
as well as of the land.

It has taught me that
I AM also the garden,
filled with germinating seeds.
To be aware of which ones
I choose to nurture,
as some are poisonous weeds.

There are places that should be
encouraged to run wild
and do their thing.
Others that benefit from the touch
of cultivation, and the beauty
and value this can bring.

It has taught me that
I can choose which seeds to plant,
but other seedlings will also come.
I must discern which to keep
or remove, and where
they've come from.

Weeds are plants that you don't want,
and didn't plant,
growing in uninvited spots.
They can resemble our
human experiences of outer scenarios,
and inner thoughts.

The weeds come in many forms:
thoughts, habits, people,
and places to name a few.
Anything that is a hindrance
to our peace of mind,
and our dreams coming true.

If the weeds are ignored,
and not dealt with, they will grow
and block out our light.
Which can prevent
the flow of growth,
which is our birthright.

Some weed's roots are near
the surface, easy to find,
and fully remove.
Others are deep,
and their removal process
not so smooth.

This is an ongoing process
of planting, nurturing
and removing in space-time.
And if we are steadfast
with our choices and actions,
we join the sublime.

Peaceful Blanket

The vast blue sky
is everywhere I go.
Like a blanket it brings comfort,
and lifts my spirit when it's low.

It has a certain quality,
that fills my heart with peace.
It comes bearing flying creatures—
eagles, seagulls, geese.

The blue sky is my greatest teacher,
it demonstrates how to live.
From a still, open present place,
with nothing but love to give.

Despite the passing
clouds and storms,
and our experiences of
changing moods and forms,

the blues sky remains untouched,
expansive, eternal and pure.
And when we embody its lessons,
we feel more free, for sure.

Home

Home is not a place,
it's a state of being.
Where man and soul meet,
and have a whole new way of seeing.

Winter Solstice Poem

Throughout the darkest
days of the year,
our darkness may arise
and cause terror and fear.

It may feel like a volcano
erupting inside.
Like there's nowhere to run to,
nowhere to hide.

The past year
is being put to rest,
a new birthing within you—
invite this new guest.

On the darkest day,
call for the Spirit of Winter to come.
To see you through,
wrap you in warmth,
and be your best chum.

In the stillness of the earth,
activity stirs in the creative void.
All is happening within you;
try not to worry or get annoyed.

Doing is not important now,
the best you can do is
rest and be still.
Release all yearnings,
do not expect or anticipate,
just chill...

Listen, what is to come will be shown.
The beginning of its dream is here.
Welcome these new beginnings,
and know lighter days are near.

Dealt Both Hands

Everybody has their stories,
that break them into pieces.
The hard ones, the tragic ones,
the ones that stink of faeces.

No one is immune to these,
we are all dealt a shitty hand.
We all have dreams that didn't turn out,
the way we hoped and planned.

Everyone also has their stories
that make them feel whole.
The fun ones, the precious ones,
the ones that fill their soul.

So we are also dealt a hand
that is generous and kind.
And by embracing both hands,
we heal our heart and free our mind.

Comfort the Discomfort

When uncomfortable,
distressing feelings appear,
it often means that
change and growth are near.

Welcome these guests;
make them some tea.
They have come to
gift you a golden key.

The key will lead you
to see with new eyes,
to a seeing were no past
can re-traumatize.

To a knowing that no one,
and no circumstance
is to blame.
It teaches that forgiveness
will release all guilt
and shame.

When the discomfort
is comfortable in having
taught you well,
you'll find a more loving,
and expanded place
within yourself to dwell.

Grief is Natures Chief

Grief is part of nature,
it's how we deal with loss.
From despair to resurrection,
it frees us from the cross.

Every loss and gain,
whether good or bad,
can set grief into motion.
The loss of what was
before the change,
can stir up deep emotion.

The more we value
what we've lost,
the more intense our grief.
We feel depressed and angry,
desperate for relief.

Coming out of denial,
and accepting our loss
is not where our work ends.
We must find, affirm,
and accept the gain it brings,
to truly make amends.

The Voices in our Head

There are two main voices
that we hear.
One comes from Love
and the other from fear.

Fear says "I'm all alone, the world's insane,
everyone including myself is fucked,
and we are all destined to die."
It makes us believe we're separate from others,
lacking, better than, less than, not enough—
it's loud and deceitfully sly.

Love says "We're never alone, we're all connected,
heaven on earth IS possible,
we are undyingly loved and WE ARE eternal."
It takes us beyond mere belief,
beyond space and time, beyond polarities and limitations
into a peaceful internal and external.

Fear speaks first and
is rather loud, and can
drown out The Voice of Love.
Through meditating, praying,
forgiving and blessing,
we can give it a gentle shove.

As we hear Love's Voice,
and become empty of all our crap
and accumulated 'knowledge,'
Love can enter and lead the way
to our graduation, from the School of Life
into the Holy College.

From this place our bodies and minds
are set free to be used to serve Love,
thus we begin to naturally play our unique part.

We are no longer in a space of wanting
and getting, or stuck in victim mode—
instead willing and able to give our heart.

Notice how,
when a loved one's form 'dies',
that Love still remains.
And that the sad shit,
the bad shit, always comes with lessons,
that ultimately help break us from the chains.

Every single thing that happened
in the past; the good, the bad, and the ugly,
was in fact all for our ultimate great.
It leads to the space where the veil gets lifted,
and we get to abide in a romantic
date with our divine mate.

The Hard Shit Helps us Excel

At times we think
we are the only one
who feels so much pain.
We think we are
the only one
that feels totally insane.

We think that *our* story,
our circumstance,
is by far the worst.
Ego thrives on
these thoughts,
to satisfy its thirst.

It looks for comparisons
to 'prove' that its pain
is 'the most awful.'
It compares it with others
and our past,
then takes these thoughts as lawful.

The reality is,
everyone has stories
that take them to hell.
These are the stories
that evoke growth,
and help us to excel.

Forgiveness Sets Us Free

I forgive the world I see.
I forgive the past me.

As I forgive the world as WE,
I see that WE are happy and free.

Free to co-create with Thee.
To share our Love with a glowful glee.

Transplant Shock

Sometimes we feel called,
to go live in another zone.
Away from where we've been,
and from all that we have known.

We could stay where we are,
and resist the change.
Or take a leap of faith,
into what at first
may seem strange.

The thoughts of relocating
can seem scary at first.
We can become distracted,
with 'fear of the worst.'

We do have the choice
to stay in the same
old mundane.
This could bring us
contentment, or it could
drive us insane.

Relocation can come
with what may feel like
an almighty thud.
Intense stress and overwhelm,
and in my case,
a goddamn flood!

Like a plant in transit,
on its way to its new spot,
fragile and vulnerable,
and restricted by its pot.

And even once
it's in the ground,
it takes time to adjust.
And establish roots,
adapt to surroundings,
and re-gain trust.

From this space,
it has the opportunity
to flourish and bloom.
As long as it's nurtured
and cared for,
and given ample room.

Like a plant in its ideal
environment, we will grow
with ease and thrive.
On finding this spot,
we can delight in the pleasures
of being alive.

Life's a Beach, Bitch!

Life's a bitch,
and then we die.
Life's a beach,
and we can fly!

Create and have Fun

We are as vast as the sky,
and as bright as the sun.
We have come as humans
to create and have fun.

Here on earth we have two
extremely important points of view.
One knows the bigger picture,
the other is personal to me and you.

Getting Drunk on Life and High on Nature

Drinking booze and
getting high on drugs,
was great fun for awhile.
Enhanced confidence, more laughter,
wildness, naughtiness—
it made me dance and smile.

What's more it allowed me
to see and experience
strange altered states.
As well as see beauty,
feel wonderment
and discover my many traits.

Partaking in the
various, tantalising,
big kid sweets,
briefly made life more fun
and inspired me
to explore new streets.

However, these substances
that get you high, have a tendency
to also get you low.
The opposite of these fun feeling states
is usually what follows,
from what I know.

A vicious cycle of depending
on the substance
to get you back up again.
As a means to get you out
of the downward spiral,
or at least to numb the pain.

These days I have found more ultimate
ways to feel confident, get relief,
enjoy altered states and have fun.
These days I get drunk on life
and high on nature,
which works for me. Win – Won!

By having a deep connection
with nature, the cycles, trees
and the vast blue sky,
and by reaching deep
within myself to ask questions,
who, what, where and why,

I have a deeper sense of
who I AM and feel more at ease,
as a unique part of the Mystery.
I feel supported and guided in my
journey to wholeness, through
healing and integrating my history.

I have experienced getting higher
and more blissful,
while totally sober.
And the real beauty is,
there are no negative side effects
and no sign of a hangover.

Preventing the low
and striving for the high,
are not the end all goals.
As these poles are here
to teach us, to hear
the whispers of our souls.

I needed both extremes,
the highs and lows,
that drink and drugs gave me,

so I could see the greatness
of sobriety and be able
to choose accordingly.

A Fresh Point of View

Transformation is death of the old
and birth of the new.
A whole new way of being,
with a fresh point of view.

A physical death is a
metamorphosis of form.
In daily living it's a shift
from what was norm.

The old me was
more sad and mad.
The new me is
more happy and glad.

I used to pay attention
to what was lacking and wrong.
Stuck in old patterns,
feeling I didn't belong.

Grief, anger, fear, guilt
and low self-esteem,
crushed my sense of peace and joy,
and my ability to dream.

Now instead of focusing on
what's wrong and
needs to change about me,
I turn my attention
to what's right,
and how I can give with glee.

Throughout the day
I place my attention on gratitude.
This has done wonders
for my outlook and attitude.

Every morning,
I make an intention
to give and allow peace and joy.
I imagine and feel
what this may look like,
a day to relish and enjoy.

I have noticed that
what I focus on and
the energy I cultivate inside,
has a huge effect on
whether or not
I'll have a rough or easy ride.

Focus on the Beauty

When you focus on what you can't do,
or don't have, you suffer.
Your experiences are mostly gray
and life is so much tougher.

When you instead focus on what you can do,
and what you do have, you see opened doors.
You dwell in the beauty of being alive,
and see the future as a gift that's all yours.

Every Moment

Every moment contains the positive
and negative of every subject.
Learn to discern well, so you may
know what to accept and what to reject.

Every moment is a fresh start,
inviting you to fully live.
Go where your soul leads you
and remember to forgive.

The Hero's Journey

I've slayed many dragons
and learned many lessons
along the way.
As my journey continues,
I'll be sure to keep
enjoying some sweet reggae.

Chill Behind the Noise

Relax, watch and listen,
as thoughts and events unfold.
In that space that's before words,
where there's nothing to uphold.

The noise of thoughts,
of sensory input,
of feelings good or bad arise—
just notice, relax,
allow and enjoy,
and look from eternal eyes.

This space is not biased
to the polarised
point of view,
because it can see,
and it knows—
both and neither are true.

From this empty
yet charged with Love
aliveness, gazing into time,
see from who you truly are;
you're both being
and becoming sublime.

The space is vast
and it settles in and around
the body and mind.
As past trapped energies arise,
they can now be free
to gently unwind.

The sounds and images
of your stories, both tragic
and epic, are released.
To allow peace and joy
to take center stage,
so you can truly enjoy life's feast.

Embrace your Deepest Fears

Loss of our loved ones and
our capabilities is inevitable.
It's important to love fully and
create moments that are memorable.

Old age, sickness and dying
come with the cycle of birth and death.
We cannot escape these truths, but
we can taste eternity in our breath.

Exploring our Almighty Planet

Curiosity and the call to
adventure, has taken me
to many places.
I've looked upon the
beauty of our land, and
into the eyes of many faces.

Travelling has opened my heart
and mind, and been one of
my greatest teachers.
I've met monkeys, snakes,
bobcats, owls, and a whole
bunch of other creatures.

I went looking for a place
to settle, always looking
for a place to go.
Often trekking through
the elements, of blazing heat,
rain and snow.

In the journey outwards
across the oceans,
to a far off distant land,
I met people and saw
things that made my heart
and mind expand.

So many different cultures,
different races, and
different ways of living.
But deep down we have
the same human needs.
We all need love and to be forgiving.

The Journey and the Many Destinations

Healing is a never-ending,
ongoing task.
With each layer we heal,
we remove another mask.

Desire is a never-ending
ongoing thing.
With each goal we reach,
the more our hearts can sing.

We never reach a place
of getting it all done.
But the more we heal and reach
our goals, the more we do have fun.

Keep moving towards
and through, another
layer of healing.
Keep moving towards
your desires and
enjoy that yummy feeling.

Let go of saying
"One day when..."
then I'll feel good.
Realize that in
any moment we have
control over our mood.

Happiness is not
a destination, it's a choice
we must make every day.
Despite the fact,
there is no end, and the
undesired never goes away.

Student AND Teacher

I've embarked on
shamanic journeys, where I found
guidance and openings to heal.
I now feel able to creatively
express myself, and respect
and honour how I feel.

When I express myself
through art, music, poetry and dance
and take steps towards my dreams,
I unearth more and more
of my Self, and I'm more able
to hold and understand extremes.

We all have our stories,
our messages, our methods,
to share, that can help us all heal.
Where we can honour both dark and light,
and reconnect with Love,
and with all that's real.

I am no Zen master,
I'm constantly learning,
I share what I learn and know.
We're all both student
and teacher, and together
we learn, blossom and grow.

Chapter 9
WHERE I AM NOW

2020 Vision

USA

It's the beginning of 2021
and my 40th birthday, the due date
for this book, is near.
I've written the majority of these
poems in the year 2020,
what a crazy ass year!

During this weird, intense time,
my family experienced 3 births
and 2 deaths.
It's been a year of so much fear,
uncertainty, madness, conflict—
a time for deep breaths.

2020 has been the year
of 20/20 vision. The hidden coming into
view for the world to see.
A seeing of our internal world,
our spiritual essence,
how will our future be?

In spring of 2020 I finally
put my stack of pregnancy
tests in the trash.
I made peace with the past,
accepted fear and death,
and my soul rose up from the ash.

The poem that follows I wrote in March 2020,
when the pandemic chaos
spread across our lands.
Our choices, our habits,
our attitudes, make an impact.
The world's future is in our hands.

With You

The reality of this whole situation
has reached my tummy,
my heart, my brain.
I am doing my best
to be love, send love
stay calm and sane.

I am being asked
to face the fear,
and allow my broken heart to grieve.
So that when this
crazy storm has passed,
I can step out anew and weave.

Weave a new world WITH YOU,
that takes into consideration
our shared humanity.
That provides the love, safety,
freedom and the unity
we need for our shared sanity.

Weave a new world WITH YOU,
that cares about our people,
our animals, our land.
Where there is no tweedle dee
or tweedle dumb and no need
to follow their command.

Weave a new world WITH YOU,
where we can all
feel like we belong.
Where we can freely
come together to share
our gifts and our heart's song.

Exploring the USA

In the nearly 4 years I've been
living in the US, I've visited
some cool places near and far.
Using various modes of transport,
flights, trains, our pickup truck,
our camper, our bikes, our car.

We visited Texas—went to Dallas,
and the hill country and stayed in
an RV in someone's driveway.
We visited a cave and a crazy
granite rock. We went to a
ranch for some good ol' horseplay.

I visited a sweet pal I met
in India, who lives in
Boulder, Colorado.
She took me to meet the elks
and magic mountains,
and fed me toast and avocado.

I've visited many places
here in Wisconsin
and the nearby states.
The beauty and places to
explore are endless.
So much more still awaits.

The mighty Mississippi is a 30
minute drive away,
I rode her on a fishing boat.
Then there's the Kickapoo,
great for a chilled-out
canoe float.

Gabriel and I camped
in a bunch of state parks
in our bell tent.
There are a select few
we really love,
that we often frequent.

*We went on a road trip to
New York, 20 hours each way,
in our old janky camper van.
I wrote a song to recover
from this hectic trip,
I really needed it, man!*

Roadtrip to New York - Song Lyrics

I love our camper,
it's our old new van.
First trip to New York,
'twas our epic plan.

Kitchen sink and cosy bed,
a place to lay our head.
Off we go in our camper van.
Off we go in our camper van.

First day we broke down,
we got towed away.
Stayed in the parking lot,
where dudeman let us stay.

First night was super hot,
sleep we never got.
But we were on the road again early next day,
on the road again early next day.

I love the cornfields,
along the country roads.
I love the soy beans,
there are fecking loads.

I love the summer heat,
and my freezing feet.
On these country roads.
On these country roads.

I love the interstate,
I love the semi-trucks.
I love the gas stops,
where I spend loads of bucks.

I love the pouring rain,
it's a total pain.
I can't see a thing.
I can't see a thing.

We stopped at the camp sites,
swam in the lakes and hiked.
Seen loads of wildlife,
this I really liked.

Heron, deer and chipmunks,
and lots of human punks.
On our way to New York.
On our way to New York.

New York was lovely,
but hot and buggy too.
Outings and card games,
with the AP (aged parents) crew.

Water lilies, waterfall,
trees and hammocks y'all...
Surrounded by chipmunks all day.
Surrounded by chipmunks all day.

*To singalong search 'shereen baird roadtrip to new york'
on Youtube...*

Where my Nearest and Dearest are Now

My blood relatives are
mainly split between
Scotland, Ireland and Iran.
And I have a wonderful
friend-family all over the globe,
who're also in my clan.

My mum works as a care-worker,
my bro Dave is a doctor,
Sean a stay at home dad.
My sis Orchid is a popstar.
I love to see them happy,
nothing makes me more glad.

David and Annika have given me
the gift of my niece and nephew,
Euan and Rosa.
Sean and Rebecca have gifted me
with my niece Jemma,
super hermosa.

My cousin Debbie now has
six growing kiddos,
and Karen has two.
My Iran side of the
family is expanding
there too.

We all keep in touch as best
we can, given the circumstances
these days.
Using letters, social networks,
video chats, and all the other
internet ways.

The Flowerhood Project

My journey from infertility to flowerhood
inspired me to create *The Flowerhood Project*.
Here I share tools that helped me
heal, transform and resurrect.

I offer the practices I've learned
from my mentors near and far.
And the knowledge and wisdom that led me
to find my north star.

I package these timeless practices
into *Bundles of Joy*,
for anyone in search of peace and purpose
to explore and enjoy.

To find out more visit www.theflowerhoodproject.com.

Future Plans

In these uncertain times,
it's hard to plan far off
adventures in advance.
Staying near to home is probably
where I'll be most, taking
graceful steps in this dance.

I'm blessed to be in the Driftless
area, Wisconsin, surrounded by
great people and stunning landscapes.
I live in a cute wee house with
a super nice garden, maybe
this year I'll try to grow some grapes.

Although living in the US has
its downsides and it's not
the perfect place,
for now I love where I am.
I have time, flowers
and ample space.

I'll continue to grow in love,
with my multi-talented
guy and fluffy cat.
I'm sure I'll keep up my
yoga practice and take it
far beyond the mat.

I'll likely continue working
with the locals, and
volunteering when I can.
I'll create *Bundles of Joy*
for *The Flowerhood Project,*
and go camping in our van.

Maybe I'll go visit
a tropical spot with
beaches and palm trees.
Maybe I'll get myself
a new puppy to
cuddle and squeeze.

Maybe I'll be able to
visit family
in the UK.
With the uncertainties
Of 2020, its hard to say.

I reckon 2021 is gonna be a
year of conflict, division
and change.
I reckon it will be quite
intense and possibly
even more strange.

We are the bridge generation,
to a fast approaching
new way of life.
We are learning to unite in a
world of opposing values—
a double-sided knife.

Old systems and ways of life
are breaking down,
that we must let go.
So we can create
a better world,
that has a mighty glow.

What Sustains Me

If everything I have is taken from me,
I will reach within my soul so I can see.
The Eternal candlelit flame that sets me free.
To be the light that unites you and me as WE.

In a World that Shifts

Being able to hold our joint sadness,
yet live in a place of awe, gratitude
and gladness is my gift.
Enjoying what I can do and what I do have,
is the super power I lean on,
in this world that continues to shift.

They Say Life Begins at 40

I'm still here, after 40 trips
around the sun.
It's been quite the journey,
both challenging and fun.

My travels around the world,
my interactions and my observations,
my traumas and triumphs,
together all helped build my foundations.

I'm grateful for the 'good and bad'
experiences that help me grow.
That come to teach me,
exactly what I need to know.

I'm grateful for all the people
I've met and am yet to meet.
Life is a wonderful gift—
it truly is really sweet.

I cannot predict what the future holds,
but I AM all in.
I will choose to act wisely,
and keep a joyful grin.

Oh So Thankful

Thank you

For my senses
and my ability to talk.
For my body
and my ability to walk.

For my beauty
and my ability to love.
For the guidance
I receive from above.

For the food, the water
and the air.
For my strength
and my ability to care.

For my loved ones
and all the people I meet.
For the seasons, the weather:
cold air and heat.

For my happiness, my sadness,
my joy and my pain.
For the plants, the animals,
the sun and the rain.

For art and music
and my ability to dance.
For my passionate relationships,
so full of romance.

For the different cultures and countries
I love to explore.
For the constant discoveries
of more things I adore.

Oh So Thankful...

Chapter 10
BLESSINGS TO YOU

Rooted in Love

May you be rooted in Love,
showered by sunlight above.
At home, with wings to explore,
fulfilled and happy doing what you adore.

Paint a Better View

May you learn to let go,
and give thanks with ease.
And feel safe and free,
despite who agrees.

May you know you're the
blank canvas and the artist too.
You can erase and come back to blank,
and always paint a better view.

Sky and Tree

May your heart be filled with
the calm, peaceful presence
of the vast blue sky.
Regardless of the storm clouds
that are sure
to pass you by.

May you embody the traits
of a tall, strong tree.
Rooted and reaching high,
wise and filled with glee.

May you live from a place
of purity and glimmer
like the pure white snow.
May the sun shine down
on you and lift your
spirit when it's low.

May you bloom into your
flower and bear the fruits
you came to share.
May you flow effortlessly
like a river, following your
dreams if you dare.

Resources

The Flowerhood Project was created to support people on their journey to peace, purpose and power, so they can enjoy and express their ever expanding potential. It was born from the seed of transformation that came from my journey from 'infertility to flowerhood.'

The project provides 'Soul Seed Support' by giving folk the tools to navigate life's inevitable storms. It aims to enable people to find their ground, live their legacy and create a life they love.

I create *Bundles of Joy* for this project. They contain the timeless practices that have brought joy back into my life. They are comprised of the tools and wisdom I've gathered from my travels around the globe, my personal inward journey and my intensive study, training and research.

Every bundle is full of vital nutrients required for divine unfoldment. Each bundle helps cultivate the soil of our soul, and feeds the seed of our sacred heart, so we may grow and bloom over and over again.

As of the writing of this book the *Wee Wellness Bundle (Nourish body, mind & spirit)* is ready to be enjoyed. This foundational bundle helps to:

- Reduce stress and anxiety
- Get grounded and centred
- Gain greater peace and joy
- Gain greater clarity and direction

- Release and rejuvenate
- Gain more self-awareness
- Feel more present and connected

It includes guided instruction in yoga, Tai Chi, mediation, journalling, breath techniques, healing songs, free form dance, energy cleansing and more.

Other bundles such as the *Menstrual Moon Bundle* (helping women ride the waves of their female ocean) and the *Grief Relief Bundle* (helping people navigate grief with grace) are coming soon.

To find out more visit:
www.theflowerhoodproject.com

Be sure to:

- Download the *Live Your Soul's Goals* FREE Meditation
- Explore the *Bundles of Joy*
- Get inspired by the blog posts
- Share your thoughts and YOUR stories with me...

Hugs + blooms
Shereen xxx

Acknowledgments

Special thanks goes to my wonderful husband Gabriel Newton Simmons for his patience and encouragement; for his ability to help me re-gain clarity when I lost direction; for being a sounding board for my ideas and giving me genius feedback; for reading and editing my work and for designing my book cover and the visuals and layout of my book. Thank you for helping me make this dream come true. You ARE a fantastic multi talented master.

To Kailean Welsh for being the first to set eyeballs on these pages. For taking the time to edit my words and give me much needed feedback. I am blessed to have you as neighbour, soul guide, friend. Thank you.

Thanks to Eileen McClusky who every time I see, when visiting friends and family in Ireland, always asks, "Have you written that book yet?" Thank you Eileen, I often heard your voice in my head asking this question. It was a great motivator to actually do it.

To my brother David Baird who recently reminded me I was turning 40 soon, thanks Dave! He also reminded me that I had planned to write a book for when that happened, and wondered if I was on it or not. I had no idea you remembered, and knowing you were waiting in anticipation helped inspire me to get it done. Thanks!

Thanks to my work colleagues Jean Ramage and Susan Turner. And to Sylvia Lawrie, for appreciating my poems and encouraging me to write more. Thank you!

Thank you to the Driftless Writing Center crew (and classmates) for the inspiring courses and classes.

Thank you to Kelly Notaras at kn literary arts and Reid Tracy at Hay House for all the amazing book writing tips and guidance I received via writing challenges, books, videos, and super helpful emails.

Also a huge thanks to everyone I've ever met, you touched my life in one way or another and helped me to become who I am today. Thank you.

Index of Poems

ix	Life Moves
xv	The Idea to Write this Book
2	Made in Iran in 1980
3	The Glasgow Kiss
6	My Baba Star
7	Good Ould Ballycastle Hey
10	Mysterious Dreams
14	J'ai Treize Ans
16	Driftwood Mode
17	Shaggy
19	I Want to Learn your Language
21	Picking up the Lingo
22	Discovering Yoga
23	Dubious Jobs
25	Fiesta and Siesta Time
26	Behind Bars
27	Danish Rye
28	Kundalini Surprise
32	The Sweet Mint Tea
33	Latin Boys
34	Alone with the Mice
35	Teaching English and Learning French
36	The Doom Zone
37	Mon Mari d'Algérie Abdenour
39	Loving the Rain
40	Exploring Careers in Edinburgh
41	A Pocket Full of Kisses
42	Travelling with Abdenour
46	Finding my Family in Iran
48	It was Time to Meet at Last
50	Peach Cheeks
54	Trying to Get Pregnant
55	Defeatism Evoked a Glimpse of Paradise
56	The Grassmarket Community Project

58	Meeting Angel Gabriel
60	Tuscany and the Robber in Rome
62	Dreaming New Dreams with Gabriel
63	Backpacking Travels with Gabriel
65	Happy's Hostel by the Ganges
68	From the Highest High to the Lowest Low
69	The Funeral and Letter to my Unborn Children
72	Kefah
73	I Needed a Change of Scenery
74	Fuck the Borders
75	First Month in Wisconsin
77	The Wedding Party
78	My Multimedia Masta
79	Grateful
80	We Moved to Town
82	An Unexpected Discovery
84	Super Transformational
86	Childless Mother Meets Motherless Children
87	Those Babyless Blues, No Longer our Daily News
87	Childfull, Childfree AND Free to Mother Many
89	Novice Gardener
92	Looking for Answers in Religions
94	Finding Tools and Practices that Work for Me
95	Understanding the Mystery of Time
96	Trying to Understand the Dark Cloud
96	Looking for Guidance and Courage
98	The Keys to Heal Past and Present Pain
100	Looking for my Deceased Relatives
101	Life Beyond Death
102	Finding the Middle Ground
103	Following and Trusting the Signs
104	Understanding My Purpose Progression
105	Looking Out at the World for Answers
106	Turning Inward to Find the Answers
110	The Wisdom of the Weeds
112	Peaceful Blanket

112	Home
113	Winter Solstice Poem
114	Dealt Both Hands
115	Comfort the Discomfort
116	Grief is Natures Chief
117	The Voices in our Head
119	The Hard Shit Helps us Excel
120	Forgiveness Sets Us Free
120	Transplant Shock
122	Life's a Beach, Bitch!
122	Create and have Fun
123	Getting Drunk on Life and High on Nature
125	A Fresh Point of View
126	Focus on the Beauty
127	Every Moment
127	The Hero's Journey
128	Chill Behind the Noise
129	Embrace your Deepest Fears
130	Exploring our Almighty Planet
131	The Journey and the Many Destinations
132	Student AND Teacher
134	2020 Vision
135	With You
136	Exploring the USA
138	Roadtrip to New York - Song Lyrics
140	Where my Nearest and Dearest are Now
141	The Flowerhood Project
142	Future Plans
144	What Sustains Me
144	In a World that Shifts
145	They Say Life Begins at 40
146	Oh So Thankful
148	Rooted in Love
148	Paint a Better View
149	Sky and Tree

www.ingramcontent.com/pod-product-compliance
Lightning Source LLC
Chambersburg PA
CBHW020423010526
44118CB00010B/394